Charles Shearer Keyser

Fairmount Park and the International Exhibition at Philadelphia

Vol. 2

Charles Shearer Keyser

Fairmount Park and the International Exhibition at Philadelphia
Vol. 2

ISBN/EAN: 9783337289317

Printed in Europe, USA, Canada, Australia, Japan

Cover: Foto ©ninafisch / pixelio.de

More available books at **www.hansebooks.com**

Presented by Claxton, Remsen & Haffelfinger.

CLAXTON, REMSEN & HAFFELFINGER,
PUBLISHERS, BOOKSELLERS, AND STATIONERS,
624, 626 & 628 MARKET ST., PHILADELPHIA.

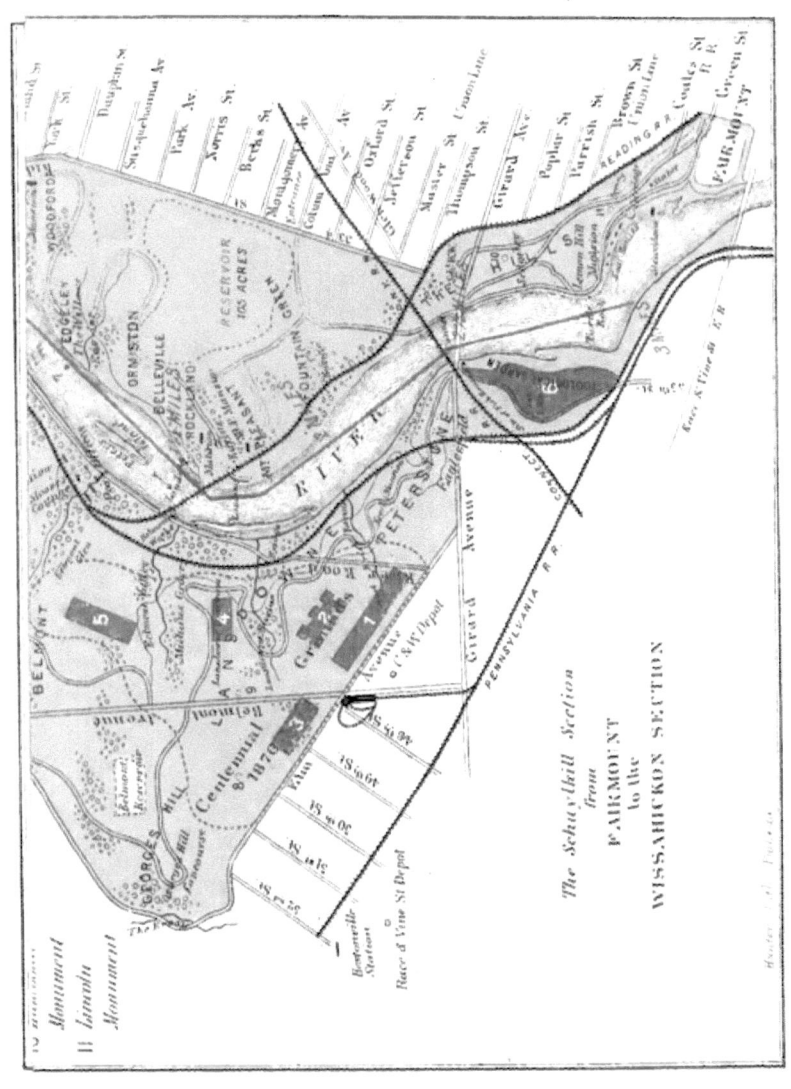

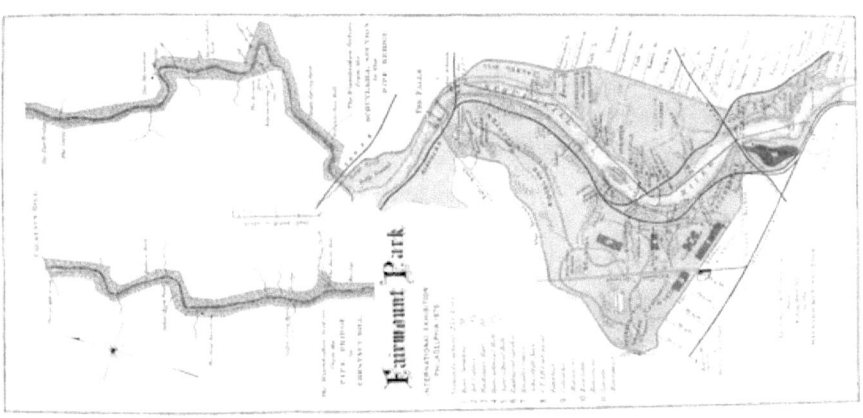

Fairmount Park

Philadelphia

AND

The International Exhibition

AT

PHILADELPHIA,

By CHARLES S. KEYSER.

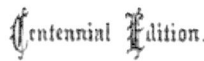

PHILADELPHIA:
CLAXTON, REMSEN & HAFFELFINGER,
624, 626 & 628 MARKET STREET.
1876.

Entered according to Act of Congress, in the year 1875 by
CLAXTON, REMSEN & HAFFELFINGER,
in the Office of the Librarian of Congress at Washington. All rights reserved.

COLLINS, PRINTER.

OFFICERS OF THE UNITED STATES GOVERNMENT.

President, ULYSSES S. GRANT, of Illinois.
Vice-President, HENRY WILSON, of Massachusetts.

Secretary of State, HAMILTON FISH, of New York.
Secretary of the Treasury, BENJAMIN H. BRISTOW, of Kentucky.
Secretary of War, WILLIAM W. BELKNAP, of Iowa.
Secretary of the Navy, GEO. M. ROBESON, of New Jersey.
Secretary of the Interior, ZACHARIAH CHANDLER, of Michigan.
Postmaster-General, MARSHALL JEWELL, of Connecticut.
Attorney-General, EDWARDS PIERREPONT, of New York.

Commissioner of Patents, J. M. THATCHER.
Commissioner of Agriculture, FREDERICK WATTS.

President of the Senate, HENRY WILSON.
Speaker of the House,

Postmaster at Philadelphia, GEO. W. FAIRMAN.

COMMITTEE OF CONGRESS ON THE EXHIBITION.

WILLIAM D. KELLEY, Pennsylvania.
GEO. F. HOAR, Massachusetts.
JOHN P. C. SHANKS, Indiana.
RODERICK R. BUTLER, Tennessee.
JOHN Q. SMITH, Ohio.
GREENBURY L. FORT, Illinois.
CHARLES CLAYTON, California.
ERASTUS WELLS, Missouri.
PIERCE M. B. YOUNG, Georgia.
JOHN T. HARRIS, Virginia.
ELISHA D. STANDEFORD, Kentucky.
RICHARD SCHELL, New York.

UNITED STATES WOMEN'S CENTENNIAL EXECUTIVE COMMITTEE.

Mrs. E. D. Gillespie, *President.*
  " John Sanders, *Vice-President.*
  " Frank M. Etting, *Secretary.*
  " S. A. Irwin, *Treasurer.*
  " John W. Forney,
  " Theodore Cuyler,
  " Richard P. White,
  " Henry Cohen,
  " H. C. Townsend,
  " Aubrey H. Smith,
  " James C. Biddle,
  " Matthew Simpson,
  " Emily R. Buckman,
  " Crawford Arnold,
  " A. H. Franciscus,
Miss Elizabeth Gratz,
  " McHenry,
Mrs. Bion Bradbury, Maine,
  " James T. Fields, Massachusetts,
  " F. W. Goddard, Rhode Island,
Mrs. W. L. Dayton, New Jersey,
  " M. E. P. Bouligny, D. C.
  " C. J. Faulkner, West Virginia,
  " Jourdain Westmoreland, Georgia,
  " Ellen Call Long, Florida,
  " M. C. Ludeling, Louisiana,
  " K. S. Minor, Mississippi,
  " Edward F. Noyes, Ohio,
  " F. R. West, Iowa,
  " J. B. Thorp, Wisconsin,
  " J. M. Crowell, Kansas,
  " S. B. Bowen, Montana,
  " Frederick MacCrellish, Cal.
  " L. C. Hughes, Arizona,
  " W. I. Hill, Idaho,
  " J. M. Washburne, Dakota,
  " M. J. Young, Texas,
  " W. S. Rand, Eastern Kentucky,
  " Worthington Hooker, Connecticut,
  " Dickinson, Missouri.

Office—903 WALNUT STREET.

THE COMMISSIONERS OF THE INTERNATIONAL EXHIBITION.

States and Territories.	Commissioners.	Alternates.
Alabama,		James L. Cooper, Huntsville.
Arizona,	Richard C. McCormick, Washington,	John Wasson, Tucson.
Arkansas,	George W. Lawrence,	George C. Dodge, Little Rock.
California,	John Dunbar Creigh, San Francisco,	Benjamin P. Kooser, Santa Cruz.
Colorado,	J. Marshall Paul, Fair Play,	N. C. Meeker, Greeley.
Connecticut,	Joseph R. Hawley, Hartford,	William P. Blake, New Haven.
Dakota,	J. A. Burbank, Bonhomme County,	Solomon L. Spink, Yankton.
Delaware,	Henry F. Askew, Wilmington,	John H. Rodney, New Castle.
Dist. Columbia,	James E. Dexter, Washington,	Lawrence A. Gobright, Washington.
Florida,	J. S. Adams, Jacksonville,	J. T. Bernard, Tallahassee.
Georgia,	George Hillyer, Atlanta,	Richard Peters, Jr., Atlanta.
Idaho,	Thomas Donaldson, Boise City,	Christopher W. Moore, Boise City.
Illinois,	Frederick L. Matthews, Carlinville,	Lawrence Weldon, Bloomington.
Indiana,	John L. Campbell, Crawfordsville,	Franklin C. Johnson, New Albany.
Iowa,	Robert Lowry, Davenport,	Coker F. Clarkson, Eldora.
Kansas,	John A. Martin, Atchison,	George A. Crawford, Fort Scott.
Kentucky,	Robert Mallory, La Grange,	Smith M. Hobbs, Mt. Washington.
Louisiana,	John Lynch, New Orleans,	Edward Penington, Philadelphia.
Maine,	Joshua Nye, Augusta,	
Maryland,	James T. Earle, Centreville,	S. M. Shoemaker, Baltimore.
Massachusetts,	George B. Loring, Salem,	William B. Spooner, Boston.
Michigan,	James Birney, Bay City,	Claudius B. Grant, Houghton.
Minnesota,	J. Fletcher Williams, St. Paul,	W. W. Folwell, Minneapolis.
Mississippi,	O. C. French, Jackson,	
Missouri,	John McNeil, St. Louis,	Samuel Hays, St. Louis.
Montana,	J. P. Woolman, Helena,	Patrick A. Largey, Virginia City.
Nebraska,	Henry S. Moody, Omaha,	R. W. Furnas, Brownsville.
Nevada,	W. Wirt McCoy, Eureka,	James W. Haines, Genoa.
New Hampshire,	Ezekiel A. Straw, Manchester,	Asa P. Cate, Northfield.
New Jersey,	Orestes Cleveland, Jersey City,	John G. Stevens, Trenton.
New Mexico,	Eldred W. Little, Santa Fé,	Stephen B. Elkins, Washington, D.C.
New York,	N. M. Beckwith, New York City,	Charles P. Kimball, New York City.
North Carolina,	Samuel F. Phillips, Washington City,	J. W. Albertson, Hartford, Perquimans Co.
Ohio,	Alfred T. Goshorn, Philadelphia,	Wilson W. Griffith, Toledo.
Oregon,	James W. Virtue, Baker City,	A. J. Dufur, Portland.
Pennsylvania,	Daniel J. Morrell, Johnstown,	Asa Packer, Mauch Chunk.
Rhode Island,	George H. Corliss, Providence,	Samuel Powel, Newport.
South Carolina,	William Gurney, Charleston,	Archibald Cameron, Charleston.
Tennessee,	Thomas H. Coldwell, Shelbyville,	William F. Prosser, Nashville.
Texas,	William Henry Parsons, Houston,	John C. Chew, New York.
Utah,	John H. Wickizer, Salt Lake City,	Wm. Haydon, Salt Lake City.
Vermont,	Middleton Goldsmith, Rutland,	Henry Chase, Lyndon.
Virginia,	F. W. M. Holliday, Richmond,	Edmond R. Bagwell, Onancock.
Washington Ter.	Elwood Evans, Olympia,	Alex. S. Abernethy, Cowlitz Co.
West Virginia,	Alexander R. Boteler, Shepherdst'n,	Andrew J. Sweeney, Wheeling.
Wisconsin,	David Atwood, Madison,	Edward D. Holton, Milwaukee.
Wyoming,	Joseph M. Carey, Cheyenne,	Robert H. Lamborn, Philadelphia.

OFFICERS OF THE COMMISSION.

President.
JOSEPH R. HAWLEY.

Vice-Presidents.

ORESTES CLEVELAND,	THOMAS H. COLDWELL,
JOHN D. CREIGH,	JOHN MCNEIL,
ROBERT LOWRY,	WILLIAM GURNEY.

Director-General.
ALFRED T. GOSHORN.

Counsellor and Solicitor.
JOHN L. SHOEMAKER, Esq.

Executive Committee.

Daniel J. Morrell,	Samuel F. Phillips,
Alfred T. Goshorn,	George B. Loring,
N. M. Beckwith,	Frederick L. Matthews,
Alexander R. Boteler,	Wm. Phipps Blake,
Richard C. McCormick,	James E. Dexter,
John Lynch,	J. T. Bernard,

Charles P. Kimball.

Committee on Commerce.

C. H. Marshall,	F. L. Matthews,
Cl. B. Grant,	Jas. L. Cooper,
A. J. Dufur,	John Mc. Neil,

John H. Rodney.

Committee on Tariffs and Transportation.

O. C. French,	James T. Earle,
Joshua Nye,	William F. Prosser,
John H. Wickizer,	Jos. M. Carey,

William H. Parsons.

Committee on Finance.

Asa Packer,
R. C. Taft,
John S. Adams,
Jas. L. Cooper,
James Birney,
Ed. R. Bagwell,
J. Marshall Paul.

Committee on Foreign Affairs.

John L. Campbell,
P. A. Largey,
Robert H. Lamborn,
John G. Stevens,
Geo. Hillyer,
Andrew J. Sweeney,
S. B. Elkins.

Committee on Opening Ceremonies.

Geo. H. Corliss,
Jno. G. Stevens,
F. W. M. Halladay,
Jas. Birney,
Geo. A. Crawford,
J. W. Albertson,
Rich. Peters.

Committee on Legislation.

Richard C. McCormick,
William F. Prosser,
Lawrence A. Gobright,
David Atwood,
Alexander R. Boteler,
Thomas Donaldson,
Saml. F. Phillips.

Committee on Classification.

Wm. P. Blake,
N. M. Beckwith,
C. P. Kimball,
John A. Martin,
Ed. Penington,
Jas. T. Earle.

Committee on Nomination of Secretaries of Departments.

Middleton Goldsmith,
Geo. H. Corliss,
John D. Creigh,
Smith M. Hobbs,
Jos. M. Carey.

Committee on History, Literature, and Population.

David Atwood,
John Lynch,
Elwood Evans,
Alex. R. Boteler,
J. Fletcher Williams,
J. A. Burbank,
Geo. C. Dodge.

Committee on Agriculture and Live Stock.

Robert Lowry,
N. C. Meeker,
Eldridge W. Little,
Andrew J. Dufur,
Robert Mallory,
Lawrence Weldon,
William Gurney.

Committee on Mines and Mining.

William Wirt McCoy,
J. D. Creigh,
J. Marshall Paul,
Thomas Donaldson,
John Wasson,
Samuel Hays,
J. P. Woolman.

Committee on Horticulture and Floriculture.

Franklin C. Johnson,
Jas. W. Virtue,
James W. Haines,
Coker F. Clarkson,
Geo. W. Lawrence,
Benj. P. Rooser,
J. C. Chew.

Committee on Fisheries and Fish Culture.

Middleton Goldsmith,
John H. Wickizer,
John C. Chew,
Elwood Evans,
Ed. Penington,
John S. Adams,
Sol. L. Spink.

Committee on Arts and Sciences.

Geo. B. Loring,
W. W. Felwell,
Wm. Haydon,
Jas. Birney,
Smith M. Hobbs,
Henry F. Askew,
Lawrence A. Gobright.

Committee on Manufactures.

Orestes Cleveland,
Wm. B. Spooner,
S. M. Shoemaker,
Danl. J. Morrell,
Wilson W. Griffith,
Geo. A. Crawford,
Henry S. Moody.

Secretary of the Commission.
JOHN L. CAMPBELL.

Office of the Commission.—No. 903 WALNUT STREET.

BUREAUS OF ADMINISTRATION.

A. T. GOSHORN, *Director-General.*

FOREIGN :—
    Direction of the foreign representation,   DIRECTOR-GENERAL.

INSTALLATION :—
    Classification of applications for space—allotment of space in Main Building—supervision of special structures,
         HENRY PETTIT.

TRANSPORTATION :—
    Foreign transportation for goods and visitors—transportation for goods and visitors in the United States—local transportation—warehousing and customs regulations,
         DOLPHUS TORREY.

MACHINERY :—
    Superintendence of the Machinery Department and building, including allotment of space to Exhibitors,   JOHN S. ALBERT.

AGRICULTURE :—
    Superintendence of the Agricultural Department, building, and grounds, including allotment of space to Exhibitors,
         BURNET LANDRETH.

HORTICULTURE :—
    Superintendence of Horticultural Department, Conservatory and grounds, including allotment of space to Exhibitors,
         CHARLES A. MILLER.

FINE ARTS :—
    Superintendence of the Fine Art Department and building, including allotment of space to Exhibitors,   JOHN SARTAIN.

THE BOARD OF FINANCE OF THE INTERNATIONAL EXHIBITION.

President,
JOHN WELSH, Philadelphia.

Vice-Presidents,
WILLIAM SELLERS, Philadelphia.
JOHN S. BARBOUR, Virginia.

Secretary and Treasurer,
FREDERICK FRALEY, Philadelphia.

Directors,

Samuel M. Felton, Philadelphia.
Daniel M. Fox, Philadelphia.
Thomas Cochran, Philadelphia.
Clement M. Biddle, Philadelphia.
N. Parker Shortridge, Philadelphia.
James M. Robb, Philadelphia.
Edward T. Steel, Philadelphia.
John Wanamaker, Philadelphia.
John Price Wetherill, Philadelphia.
Henry Winsor, Philadelphia.
Henry Lewis, Philadelphia.

Amos R. Little, Philadelphia.
John Baird, Philadelphia.
Thomas H. Dudley, New Jersey.
A. S. Hewitt, New York.
John Cummings, Massachusetts.
John Gorham, Rhode Island.
Charles W. Cooper, Pennsylvania.
William Bigler, Pennsylvania.
Robert M. Patton, Alabama.
J. B. Drake, Illinois.
George Bain, Missouri.

BUILDING COMMITTEE OF THE BOARD OF FINANCE:

THOMAS COCHRAN, *Chairman.*

JOHN BAIRD,   WM. SELLERS,
CLEMENT M. BIDDLE,   SAML. M. FELTON,
JAMES M. ROBB.

ARCHITECTS AND CONTRACTORS.

Main Exhibition Building—Architects, HENRY PETTIT and JOSEPH M. WILSON. Contractor, RICHARD J. DOBBINS.

The National Memorial (Art Gallery)—Architect, H. J. SCHWARZMANN. Contractor, R. J. DOBBINS.

Machinery Hall—Architects, HENRY M. PETTIT and JOSEPH M. WILSON. Contractor, PHILIP QUIGLEY.

The Horticultural Building—Architect, H. J. SCHWARZMANN. Contractor, JOHN RICE.

The Agricultural Building—Architect, JAMES H. WINDRIM. Contractor, PHILIP QUIGLEY.

The Building for the Government Exhibits—Architect, JAMES H. WINDRIM. Contractor, AARON DOANE.

The Building for the Woman's Department—Architect, H. G. SCHWARZMANN. Contractors, JACOB G. PETERS and JOHN ADAM BURGER.

The British Commission Buildings—Architect, THOMAS HARRIS; Assistant, THOMAS THORN. Contractor, JOHN RICE.

The Jury Pavilion—Architect, H. J. SCHWARZMANN. Contractor, LEVI KODER.

"The South," The Southern Head-quarters—Architect, H. J. SCHWARZMANN.

OFFICERS OF THE FAIRMOUNT PARK COMMISSION.

President,
MORTON McMICHAEL.

Vice-President,
JOHN WELSH.

Treasurer,
HENRY M. PHILLIPS.

Secretary,
R. W. ROBBINS.

Solicitor,
WM. H. YERKES.

Superintendent,
RUSSELL THAYER.

Commissioners,

Theodore Cuyler,	Eli K. Price,
William F. Dixey, *ex off*.	Gustavus Remak,
Robert W. Downing, "	John Rice,
Wm. H. McFadden, "	William S. Stokley, *ex off*.
A. Wilson Henszey, "	Thomas A. Scott,
James McManes,	Samuel L. Smedley, *ex off*.
Morton McMichael,	William Sellers,
Henry M. Phillips,	John Welsh.

OFFICE OF COMMISSION, 217 SOUTH THIRD STREET.

CENTENNIAL COMMITTEE

OF THE

FAIRMOUNT PARK COMMISSION.

WILLIAM SELLERS, Chairman.

SAMUEL L. SMEDLEY,	WILLIAM SELLERS,
THEODORE CUYLER,	JOHN WELSH,
GUSTAVUS REMAK,	JAMES McMANES,

ROBERT W. DOWNING.

THE NATIONAL EXECUTIVE BOARD OF THE INTERNATIONAL EXHIBITION.

COL. C. S. LYFORD, Chairman.

Department of the Treasury,
HON. R. W. TAYLOR.

Department of War,
COL. C. S. LYFORD, U. S. A.

Department of the Navy,
ADM. T. A. JENKINS, U. S. N.

Department of the Interior,
JOHN EATON, Esq.

Department of the Postal Service,
DR. C. F. McDONALD.

Department of Agriculture,
WM. SAUNDERS.

The Smithsonian Institution.
PROF. S. F. BAIRD.

PREFACE.

THE Republic of the United States having determined to commemorate the close of the first Century of its existence by an INTERNATIONAL EXHIBITION, the City which was its birth-place was appropriately selected as the site of the Exhibition.

But, for ulterior reasons also, the selection was wisely made. By a liberal provision for the health and enjoyment of her citizens, Philadelphia alone, among the cities of America, has reserved a tract of ground adequate for such an Exhibition.

If to this be added the further consideration, that the city was founded in deeds of peace, it appears necessarily and appropriately the place where our Nation's purposes of Peace should be given expression, by this assemblage of the people of the Nation, and the peoples and rulers of other nations.

And, therefore, whatever proper desire there was to assemble this vast multitude around some other altar, dear to the memory of the people — when the delegates from the States and the Congress of the nation passed into the great natural amphitheatres of this pleasure-ground, a generous preference was given to Philadelphia as the place of the great Exhibition.

The City has proved worthy of the selection; recognizing this generous preference, in unity with the States and the Nation, she completes the preparation for the first assemblage in America of the nations of the earth in the interests of peace.

Fairmount Park.

FAIRMOUNT PARK, in which the International Exhibition of 1876 will be holden, is the most extensive and in natural advantages the most attractive among the pleasure grounds of the cities of America.

It comprises over 3000 acres of ground, and is traversed by fifty miles of carriage drive, and one hundred miles of path for pedestrians and equestrians. It borders and includes the Schuylkill River and the Wissahickon, a tributary stream, and begins at Fairmount, a point on the former, distant about one and a half mile from the Centre Square of the city, and terminates at Chestnut Hill, on the latter, distance of over twelve miles.

The Schuylkill, its principal river, has an average breadth of a quarter of a mile; in some of its portions winding so as to present the appearance of broad lakes, at others showing a full silent flow for long distances. The Wissahickon is one of, if not the most remarkable of all known waters, as a type of the purely romantic in scenery. The Park has twenty small streams, tributaries of these, with four mineral springs, and one hundred and fifty of pure cold water, in some places found bubbling through the greensward, in others trickling down the rocky hillsides. It has every variety of scenery—cascades, green and wooded islands, meadows, uplands, lawns, rocky ravines, high hill summits, and open fields. It contains two hundred thousand native, many foreign trees, shrubs, and vines, and a great variety of indigenous flowers. It has also the remains of the primeval forests as they stood in the days of the aborigines, and old historic mansions which connect the present era with the days prior to the Revolution, and preserve the memory of the greatest statesmen, jurists, and heroes of America.

The most prominent object near the main entrance of the Park is an ancient hill, formed into a reservoir. An entrance for pedestrians passes along its lower side, under a bridge, into a garden, in which the principal water-works of the city are located. The main entrance of the Park for equestrians, pedestrians, and carriages passes along its upper side. The hill is terraced, with easy ascents, and planted with trees.

Its name, originally "Faire-mount," embraces as well all the near objects as itself; the Bridge, the Water-works, the Dam, the Landing, the Garden; and in the formation of the Park it was extended to the entire grounds. Fairmount has, with its first ownership, a noteworthy association with the founder of the State. His eye contemplated it as his place of residence; this purpose was not executed, but it assures us of a taste, which in this, as in all other things, meets the most unreserved approval, and among the men of those days, there is no one with whom our Fairmount could be more appropriately associated. The Founder was, with all beside for which we hold his name in veneration, a lover of nature; for himself, having most pleasure in the country life. He gave the hill beyond its first name, by causing a vineyard to be planted there. He designed Philadelphia to be and remain "a green countrie towne;" and laid out its four open squares to be so forever; he would have even kept the borders of the Delaware a grassy slope, and called his State *Sylvania*.

THE FAIRMOUNT BRIDGE,

Which crosses the river here, winds along the lower side of the hill, forming on both sides of the river the Park's southern boundary. It is a massive structure of granite and iron, with roadways on its upper and lower chord. Its entire length, with the approaches, is 2730 feet; it crosses the river by a single span of 348 feet; the roadway of each chord, which is 32 feet broad, has outside footways 8 feet broad; the width of the bridge from centre to centre of each is 50 feet; the upper chord of the bridge crosses the entrance at a height of 30 feet over it, with spans 60 feet apart, and crosses the Pennsylvania Railroad at that height on the opposite shore; the towers and abutments are of mason granite. It is the fourth bridge which has crossed at this place; the first was a floating bridge, of which an engraving remains, made in 1796; this was succeeded by a single span wooden structure of graceful proportions, once described as a scarf thrown across the river.[1] It was destroyed by fire Sept. 1, 1838. Its successor was the wire-bridge—cables suspended over two granite columns on each side the river.[2] The present bridge was commenced in the early part of 1873, and opened July 4, 1875. It was designed by STRICKLAND KNEASS; iron work by the KEYSTONE BRIDGE CO.; masonry, WM. M. WILEY, of Lancaster; it replaced the former bridge without any interruption of travel. The bridge commands a view of the city and the Park to Belmont and river, and first glimpses of the Exhibition Buildings.

[1] Built by Lewis Wernwag in 1813.
[2] Built by Charles Ellet, and opened Jan. 2, 1842.

THE FAIRMOUNT WATER WORKS.[1]

Philadelphia was first supplied with water from the Schuylkill in 1799; these works were commenced in 1812, and were put in operation three years afterwards.

They were originally run by steam-power. The Dam was commenced in 1819. Water flowed over it for the first time in 1821, and in the fall of 1822 the first wheel started and the use of steam was discontinued. The building in which these steam-engines were erected is still standing, and since 1835 has been occupied as a saloon. Adjoining the saloon is

[1] During the occupancy of Philadelphia, Sept. 26, 1776, to June 18, 1778, the British had pickets in the Robert Morris Mansion. Their line of redoubts began in Kensington and extended by Bush Hill, terminating at Fairmount. The redoubts were visible on the Fairmount Hill until the completion of the last reservoir.

THE main carriage road, after passing Fairmount, descends into an open plaza; in which are, a fountain, a pavilion which covers a mineral spring, the Park carriage stand, the barge houses of the Schuylkill Navy, the Steamboat Landing, and the Statue of Lincoln.

THE LINCOLN STATUE.

This statue was dedicated on the 22d September, 1871, in the presence of a great concourse of citizens. It is of bronze, and represents the President seated. The right hand holds a pen, the left the Emancipation Proclamation. The height of the statue is nine feet six inches. The pedestal is granite, with two four-sided plinths; on the faces of the upper are crossed flags, the United States arms, the arms of the State, and crossed swords; on the faces of the lower are these inscriptions:—

To
ABRAHAM LINCOLN,
From a grateful people.

Let us here highly resolve
That the government of the people,
By the people and for the people,
Shall not perish from the earth.

I do order and declare
That all persons held as slaves
Within the States in rebellion
Are and henceforth shall be
Free!

With malice towards none,
With charity for all,
With firmness in the right, as God gives us to see the right,
Let us finish the work we are in.

THE FOUNTAIN.

This fountain occupies the site of an ancient fish-pond; in this pond were many goldfish which found their way into the Schuylkill by canals dug through the plaza when the grounds were, some years ago, given over to speculative purposes. The fish now in the inclosure of the fountain are the lineal descendants of these, and were some years ago taken from the Schuylkill, where they have formed a very numerous colony.

THE MINERAL SPRING.

This spring has from a very remote period enjoyed a considerable reputation for the strengthening properties of its waters; they are chalybeate.

On summer mornings, visitors are found around this spring, sometimes in sufficient numbers to recall the scenes at the more popular waters of Saratoga and the Badens.

THE SCHUYLKILL RIVER.

An ancient fisherman of the State in Schuylkill, thus describes to the writer this river as it was until the building of the Fairmount Dam and the removing of their old fishing house from the Park limits in 1822. On the east bank, from Fairmount to the Falls, there were bold rocks—two remarkable ones at the Hills, and one at the Columbia Bridge. On the west bank,[1] above the Fishing House, there was also a large rock; but, for the most part, the shore on that side was shelving to the river. There were more islands than now, among them was one above the Fishing House, thickly wooded, a favorite resort for the people; a narrow channel ran between it and the shore, and the trees on the island and along the shore interlaced their branches. The island known as Peters, at the Columbia Bridge, was larger. The feature which characterized most noticeably both the shores and the island was

---

[1] Nothing can equal the beauties of the *coup-d'œil* which the banks of the Schuylkill present in descending towards the south from the Falls to Philadelphia.—*Chastellux* (1780).

a great profusion of wild flowers, coloring them with their various hues. On the bluffs of the east bank, and along the ridges of the west, the landscape-gardeners on the country-seats had changed the natural characteristics of the grounds to the formal style of the times, but between these and the river all was untouched.

The river was then subject to the rise and fall of the tide; this made at places, where its bed was irregular and rocky, falls or descents; there at the going out of the tide it ran or fell with some violence and shock, giving rise to one of its Indian names, "The Noisy Water;" this ceased with the building of the Dam, and it then assumed its present broad, even, silent flow; this, and the submerging of some of the islands by the back-water, and a decrease in the size of those which remain, are the most marked features of the change from that early time. Portions of the bluffs, also, are concealed by the bridges which now span the river. Other portions of them have been used by quarrymen, but many of those old landmarks—bluffs, islands, and shelving shores—are still clearly traceable; and the placid beauty of its now broader and quiet waters is even more attractive than its rapid flow before the erection of the Dam. The grounds of the old country-seats have lost much by neglect, yet they have also gained by the removal of the narrower, separate designs and road-ways of the individual owner, and their absorption into broad general effects and avenues for the people. The flowers are also revealing themselves again along the shores, while the grounds around the old mansions, so dear to our remembrance, have been preserved and are being restored, so that this beautiful river, then so attractive, is returned again with a heightened effect to the condition of its earlier era. As one of its names[1] evidences that it was to the aborigines, so it is to us also,

---

[1] Called by the aborigines "Ganshewehanna," the noisy stream; and "Manayunk," our place of drinking. The present is a Holland name, originating with the first settlers.

"our place of drinking," and it is to the popular determination to retain it for this purpose we owe mainly the preservation of its shores as a great public pleasure-ground. And surely never before in the world had a people in any city, even in the remote East or classic lands, such "flower-crowned bowl" from which to drink, as is this river; nor ever before beautified a common necessity of life with so perfect a measure of all its romance and poetry.

THE SCHUYLKILL NAVY.

"The healthful and manly exercise of rowing."

Boating on the Schuylkill begins with the light canoe of the Indian. From this rude though graceful origin, and following close upon it, came the boats which composed the squadron of "the Colony in Schuylkill," and the bateaux of Fort St. David's. This squadron, called also "the Schuylkill Navy," was composed of the "Shirk" and the "Fly;" their successors, under an act passed in 1762, for the augmentation of "the Navy in Schuylkill," were the "Manayunk" and "Washington," respectively fifteen and seventeen feet long, they were built of mulberry timber, with ash oars; these remained until 1822 within the Park limits. The barge of the Founder, also, sometimes appeared on these waters; it was one of much stateliness—had a regular crew and officers—pulled six oars, and bore the broad pennant with the Proprietary's arms. The Founder had enough of the great Admiral's blood in his veins to delight in boats, for this barge he always manifested much solicitude, and in a letter to James Logan, whose words go straight to the true waterman's heart, he says: "But above all dead things, my barge; I hope nobody uses it on any account, and that she is kept in a dry dock, or, at least, covered from the weather." After these came the pioneer clubs, which preceded the present organization; the first of which, the "Blue Devil," was organized 1833. Its first barge, the "Blue Devil" participated in the earliest regatta of which we have record (Nov. 12, 1835). In this regatta, the Ariel, Nymph, Dolphin, and another were entered, four-oared barges; and the Cleopatra, Falcon, Sylph, Blue Devil, Metamora, Aurora, and Imp, eight-oared barges. The organization of the present Schuylkill Navy was effected in 1858, and the first regatta took place in 1859. It then numbered eleven clubs, the Bachelors, University, Keystone, Camilla, Independent, Undine, Neptune, Chebucto, Quaker City, Nautilus, and Excelsior; and twenty boats, the Linda, Iris, Gazelle, Ariel, Lucifer, Arab, Spree, Atlanta, Gipsey, Naiad, Whisper, Undine, Fawn, Irene, Menanka, Cygnet, Spider, Nautilus, Intrepid, and Falcon. It is now, both in its appointments and organization, the most complete association devoted to rowing in the world. It numbers ten clubs and sixty-seven boats. It has four hundred and seventy-one members; and its boats and houses are valued at $100,000.

In addition to the regattas, and usual daily exercise, the clubs of this Navy sometimes make long excursions. One of these was made in 1861, by the Malta Club, on the Susquehanna to Havre de Grace; another, to Easton, by the Pickwick Club, to which the Crescent is the successor. In May, 1859, the Bachelors Barge Club made an excursion on the Delaware River and Delaware and Raritan Canal to New York. And a double scull outrigger, the Fawn, of the Undine Club, made the same excursion, September 10, 1867; distance 105 miles, rowing time eighteen hours.

An entire revolution is going on in the class of boats used by the Navy, which will have a very important bearing on the future of this organization and boating generally. The shell is superseding the others. This means necessarily an advance in the science itself, and, with the river best adapted in this country on account of its almost uniform quiet at all seasons, its width, length, and freedom from traffic, may ultimately render this organization the universal centre for test trials of skill and endurance. These trials in England, and to a great extent in this country, concentrate an interest which may be called national.

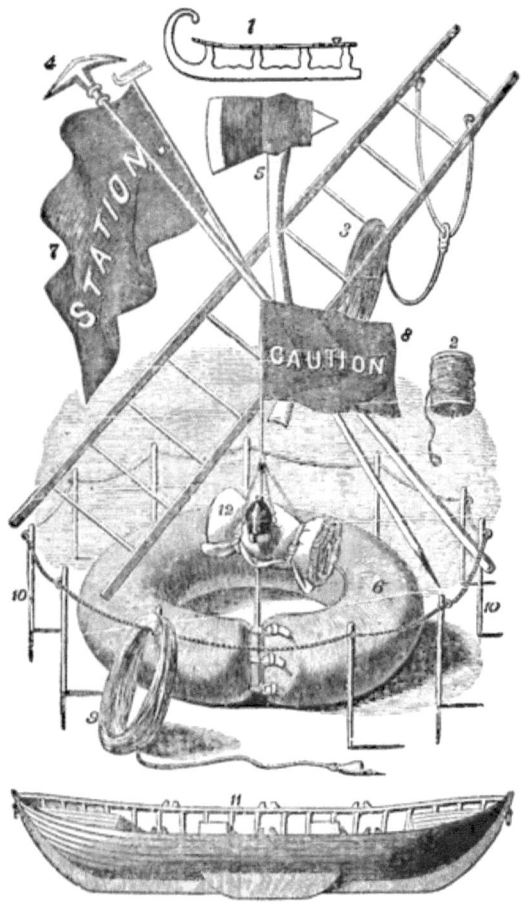

THE PHILADELPHIA SKATING CLUB.

Incorporated 1861. Its objects are improvement in the art of skating, and securing efficiency in the use of, and proper apparatus to rescue persons breaking through the ice. The active members in 1864 were 260, honorary 10; they now number 350.

The house occupied by the Club is forty feet front by sixty feet in depth, two stories high, built of fine gray stone, and pointed. The building is of Italian architecture, and ornamented with a handsome cupola and flagstaff fifty-five feet high. The roof is covered with slat-work, and encircled with a secure and handsome railing, and has a cupola.

The first story, forty by sixty feet, is appropriated entirely for the life-saving apparatus and barge boats. The second story is divided as follows: A Ladies' or Reception Room, fronting on the water, with a Retiring Room, the Members' Room, Executive Committees' Room, and the Board of Surgeons' Room. This room is furnished with all kinds of the most approved apparatus for rescuing and restoring suspended respiration to persons drowning, consisting of—1. Badges; 2. Cord and reels; 3. Ladders; 4. Hooks; 5. Axes; 6. Life-floats; 7. Station flags; 8. Caution flags; 9. Life-lines; 10. Air-hole guards; 11. Boats; 12. Blankets, grapnels, and drags. The boats are made of cedar, small and light, about one hundred pounds in weight, and sixteen feet long[1] (see plate). The records of the Society show that two hundred and sixty-one lives have been saved through its instrumentality. Among its members is Col. James Page, who still, as he was half a century ago, is our most graceful skater, and linked with all the boyish memories of the passing generation.

---

[1] All these are placed at the disposal of the Commission by the Society.

Leaving the Plaza, the road ascends[1] the second of these hills, the site of Robert Morris's home, known of late years as Lemon Hill.[2]

Near the mansion which stands there,[3] and of which this is a drawing, the road passes on the left hand two Tulip Poplars and Pines, which

---

[1] It passes on the right hand four deciduous (swamp) cypress-trees, the remains of a large group.

[2] Called formerly "Old Vineyard Hill." The Founder sent a skilful gardener from France and introduced the culture of foreign grapes here, but with no great success. His contributions to the attractions of nature should also be mentioned: he sent from England walnuts, hawthorns, hazels, and fruit-trees; a great variety of rare seeds and roots from Maryland, also some panniers of trees and shrubs; and directed by his letters that "the most beautiful wild flowers of the woods" should be transplanted to his grounds.

[3] The late Mr. Pratt, a merchant of this city, was building here in the summer of 1796, probably erecting this mansion.

stood there during the Revolution; and are noble representatives of the primeval forest. The general character of the grounds remains unchanged. The forms of the superb terraces are still visible, although the rare flowers, vases, and statues once there are gone. There is a good view of Fairmount, the river, and the city from the hall-door of this mansion.

In the old house,[1] which stood here, Robert Morris resided from 1770 to 1798, twenty-eight years—a period embracing the Revolution and the

Presidency of Washington. He had a fine mansion in the city, but his house on these grounds was his home; winter and summer his hours of rest and enjoyment were passed here. In 1776 (Dec. 29) he wrote to Baltimore, where Congress, having fled from the city, was sitting: "I have always been satisfied with Philadelphia and the Hills. At the same time I have been constantly prepared; my things packed up, horses and carriages ready at any moment; I dine at the Hills to-day, and have done so every Sunday. Thus, you see, I continue my old practice of mixing business with pleasure; I ever found them useful to each other."

[1] The cut is a fac-simile of Robert Morris's home, from a painting by the late Samuel Breck.

And when the evil days came, in which he had no pleasure, still he clung to this place. From "the Hills" he wrote (Feb. 8, 1798): "It is the only place of calmness and quiet my foot was in all day yesterday."

ROBERT MORRIS.

Robert Morris was the representative of the capitalists of the Colonies, the most honorable, and the most unfortunate. As such, he has left, of his public life, three records, intelligible to his own and to after generations. His first record is a letter, a short extract from which follows; it was written on these grounds.

From the Hills on Schuylkill:—

"July 20th, 1776.

. . . "It is the duty of every individual to act his part in whatever station his country may call him to, in a time of difficulty, danger, or distress."

His second record is his signature to the great Declaration, and the pledge of his financial abilities and his private fortune to the cause of the Colonies.

His third record is the ledger of his counting-house and the folios of the Government, of which he was the Treasurer from the year 1781 to the close of the Revolution. These show that he held the army together, from hour to hour, through the Revolution, by the credit of his individual name.[1]

Among the items of the accounts of this faithful steward are some which illustrate the whole. 1779 and 1780 were the most distressing

---

[1] "The individual notes of Robert Morris circulated *as cash* through the Colonies."—*Chastellux* (1780).

years of the war. On a pressing occasion, during this period, Washington communicated to Judge Peters the condition of the public stores: his army was without cartridges, those in the men's boxes were wet; if attacked, retreat or destruction was inevitable. In this emergency the Board of War, of which Judge Peters was Secretary, was powerless; all the lead accessible was exhausted, even to the lead spouts of the houses, and the Board was then offering for it, without obtaining any, the equivalent in paper of two shillings in specie a pound. Judge Peters showed Washington's letter to Mr. Morris, who was with others at a reception at Don Juan Mirailles's, the Spanish Minister.

By a fortunate concurrence, a privateer had that day arrived at the wharf at Philadelphia, one-half consigned to Mr. Morris. He said to Judge Peters, one-half of the Holker's cargo is consigned to me; she is at the wharf, take the one-half of the unfortunate supply — it is ninety tons of lead; the owners of the other half are standing there; get theirs also. But, said Judge Peters, they will make no further advances to the government. Then, said Mr. Morris, I take myself their portion and deliver it to you. The arrangement was at once made. That night one hundred hands were employed. Before morning a supply of cartridges was on its way to the army.

Again, December, 1776, from his broken army on the Delaware, Washington wrote that without specie an offensive movement could not be made. This letter was sent by a confidential messenger to Mr. Morris; but it seemed impossible, in the general confusion and flight of the citizens, to raise the sum required. Among his acquaintances, however, was a cautious but straightforward capitalist. To this man he made his wishes known. What is the security for this sum? said the capitalist. My note and my honor, was the answer of Morris. On that security I will loan the money, was his answer. With this money Washington was enabled safely to cross the Delaware and secure the decisive result at Trenton.

At the most critical period of our nation's early history, 1781, Judge Peters, Robert Morris, and Washington were together at the Headquarters of the Army, on the North River. Washington received on that occasion a letter from the Count De Grasse, announcing his determination to remain in the West Indies with the French fleet. Washington read the letter, which destroyed at one blow his plan of operations on the city of New York, and resolved at once on the expedition to Virginia. Turning to Judge Peters, he said, What can you do for me? With money, everything; without it, nothing—was the brief reply, as he turned with an anxious look to Morris. Let me know the sum you desire, said the Patriot Financier. Washington's estimates were made that night. Morris placed, within the required time, the amount of the estimates in Judge Peters's hands—the army moved. The result was the surrender of Lord Cornwallis, at Yorktown—the successful close of the war for the Independence of the Colonies.

Judge Peters gives the requirements of Washington, for this brilliant and final effort, as follows: "Seventy to eighty pieces of battering cannon, and one hundred of field artillery, were completely fitted and sent on for service in three or four weeks, progressively; and the whole together, with the expense of provisions for, and pay of, the army was accomplished on Mr. Morris's credit, which he pledged in his notes, which were all paid, to the amount of one million four hundred thousand dollars. Assistance was, 'tis true, afforded by Virginia and other States, from the merit whereof I do not mean to detract. We had no money in the War Office chest; the Treasury was empty; and the expedition would never have been operative, had not most fortunately Mr. Morris's credit and superior exertions and management supplied the indispensable *sine qua non.*"[1]

These are items in the account of this faithful steward. And when it is considered that bills of credit finally would buy nothing; that cattle died on the road to the army for want of public money to buy provender; that the Colonies themselves ceased to comply with the requisitions upon them; that clothes for the soldiers were sold to pay the more suffering needlewomen who made them—we may estimate how constant were those drains upon his private fortune, and how large was their aggregate.

From the spirit and the word of that letter from "the Hills," Robert Morris, from the first to the last, never swerved. The signature which he appended to the Declaration was repeated again and again to notes which were met as they matured, and which amounted to millions; but this expenditure of his private fortune, princely as it was, was not the measure of his service. The folios of the Government show a reduction of expenses, while its finances were in his hands, from eighteen to four millions annually, and this still was not the full measure of his service. These pledges of the individual wealth of a man, who was himself the national coffer, *inspired* as well as sustained the country; this completes the measure of his services, for this he was called in his day the right arm of the Revolution.

[1] Judge Peters to Alexander Garden, Esq., Belmont, Dec. 20, 1821, MS.
John Adams was for some time his near neighbor. His house was at Bush Hill.

The main carriage road passes next over the third of these hills, formerly known as

SEDGELEY PARK.

This portion of the grounds, a tract of thirty-four acres, was purchased by contributions from citizens of Philadelphia, and presented to the city, in 1857, for a public park and to preserve the purity of the Schuylkill water. The acceptance of this gift by the city was followed by its immediate dedication to the people for their use and enjoyment. A tasteful little structure stands here, formerly a porter's lodge, for a mansion which stood here overlooking the river; the view from this portion of the grounds gives the bridges—the nearer the Girard Avenue, and the farther the Railroad Bridge—the Solitude on the opposite shore with its fine grove, and the site of the old fishing-house of the State in Schuylkill. Here are found some trees worthy of notice—the most remarkable one the road passes on the right hand. The hill breaks off in bluffs along the margin of the river, and forms a ravine through which a little rivulet runs; and along whose border violets, spring beauties, quaker ladies, and the May apple, the first spring offerings, are found. This hill is about eighty feet above the river—it has been selected as the site for a monument to Humboldt. The most notable object in Sedgeley is an earthwork, yet traceable, constructed during the late war as part of the system of defences for Philadelphia; it is on its highest elevation near the bridge. There is also on these grounds another relic of those days—

THE GIRARD AVENUE BRIDGE

replaced a wooden structure on the same site. It was entirely rebuilt, from the foundation of the piers. It was begun the 12th day of May,

1873, and completed the 4th day of July, 1874. It is 1000 feet long, and 100 feet wide; has a central roadway paved with granite blocks for carriages and car-tracks, 67 feet wide, footpaths on either side $16\frac{1}{2}$ feet wide, paved with slate, with white marble borders. The bridge is constructed of iron and stone, with bronze ornamentation. It has five spans, three river, and two shore, the former each 197 feet long, the latter each 137 feet long. The bridge rises from the east to the west abutment arch four feet grade; the distance from the surface of the water to the western end pier is an average of 23 feet. The abutments are 108 feet long, and 18 feet wide; they are of granite, laid on a solid rock foundation, 25 to 30 feet below the water surface. The lines of the piers are 120 feet long and 10 feet wide at the water surface, and 113 feet long and $8\frac{1}{2}$ feet wide under the coping, with elliptical chords. The iron work at the arch abutment is 24 feet above the masonry, the roadway being an average of 50 feet above the water surface. The railings are panelled with rich designs in bronze—the Phœnix, the Eagle, and the cotton plant alternating; the bridge is lighted with 12 candelabra of graceful design. Designers and Constructors, CLARK, REEVES & Co.

GRANT'S COTTAGE.

The small frame house which stands on these grounds was brought here, at the close of the late war, from City Point. It was there occupied by General Grant as his headquarters.

The main carriage road gives a broad view of the river as it gradually descends the hill to the Girard Avenue Bridge.

THE SCHUYLKILL WATER WORKS.

These Works, brick buildings in the Egyptian order, stand in a ravine just beyond this bridge; they are operated by steam. Their pumping capacity is 22,947,000 gallons per diem. The storage room in the reservoir, attached to the Works, is 9,800,000 gallons. The Connecting Railway Bridge crosses here. The road unites railroad lines for all sections of the nation. Near its east abutment is

THE TUNNEL.

The hill, which forms the farther side of the ravine in which these works are situated, terminates in a huge rock, which rises abruptly from the water's edge to the height of sixty feet; this rock, Promontory Point, is tunnelled through for a road along the river. The tunnel is one hundred and forty feet long, forty-one feet wide, and twenty-two feet nine inches high, and is throughout solid natural rock, without any lining whatever; it is elliptical in section, with straight sides and an arched roof. It was begun October, 1870, and finished June, 1871.

THE STATE IN SCHUYLKILL.

"Atte the leest he hath his holsom walke and mery at his ease a swete ayre of the swete savoure of the meede floures that makyth him hungry, and if the angler take fysshe surely there is noo man merier than he is in his spyryte."[1]

A tract[2] beginning at Solitude, and extending to the Sweet Brier Mansion, was formerly called "Egglesfield." Its first owner, a contemporary with the aborigines, was one William Warner,[3] an amiable and worthy man, and a member of the durable order of plain colors and rectitude. Nearly a century and a half ago (the year 1732), certain gentlemen, fol-

[1] Book of St. Albans.
[2] The estate was of late years the property of the Borie family, of Philadelphia.
[3] William Warner died Sept. 12, 1794.

lowers of "Walton," leased one acre of this tract; this they inclosed with a worm-fence.

For the ground, they formally delivered on a large pewter plate to William Warner, as a yearly rental, every spring, "three sun perch fish," and they elevated him to the dignity of a Baron, so that he might be the more worthy to receive the service of this feudality. After securing the title to the one acre of ground, it is said they got together some of the same Indian chiefs who signed "the Treaty" with the Founder, and as they had no Elm trees, they sat them down under their Black Walnut trees.

They smoked many calumets of peace with them, and entered into a similar solemn treaty for the privilege of hunting and fishing at all times forever along these shores. The consideration for the privilege they ladled out to these swarthy granters from a large bowl, and if the courses of their signatures along the parchment were devious ones, it would assure, what we might credit without the assurance, that no advantage was taken of them in the consideration. The preliminaries thus arranged, these fishermen, with their sturdy arms, hewed down trees enough and erected themselves a hut. Then they constituted themselves, by letters patent, a colony, by name "The Colony in Schuylkill." For the Colony they elected a Governor, to order its general affairs; a Sheriff, to serve writs of execution on the feathered denizens of the forest and the restive trespassers of the stream; a Coroner, to view their inanimate forms after execution and pronounce them dead and edible. Having done all this, they then sat down to fish; and what is an incredible thing to all but fishermen, they continued to sit there ninety years; at the end of this time, one morning their spirits became sorrowful, their corks rested on the water motionless. Looking around them, they perceived that civilization had been advancing steadily towards them, while they had been unconsciously sitting there, and that "an anathema"[1] fatal to fishermen had been levelled against them at Fairmount; a barrier through which their faithful fish could reach their hooks no longer. Then they got up, and, carrying their house with them, followed the course of the finny tribe further down the stream, and beyond the Park limits, where they and the house still remain, but where the limits of this book forbid us to follow them. When these patient fishermen sat down to fish, one hundred and forty years ago, from the old Independence Hall to the borders of this Park was one unbroken wilderness. The canoe of the Indian was still there, and the deer drank at the borders of this stream; now, a city,[2] with nearly a million of people, covers this whole area; the silver shad come to them no more, the rock more and more rarely, and the memory of the one trout fish they caught in this stream, a century ago, grows dimmer every hour, but they still sit quietly beside its borders, and they say to us, in their master's words, "No life is so happy and so pleasant as the life of a well-governed angler, for when the lawyer is swallowed up in business, and the statesman is preventing or contriving plots, then he possesses himself in quietness;" and it is truly said of angling, what Dr. Boteler said of strawberries, "Doubtless God could have made a better berry, but doubtless God never did." And so, if we may be judges, God never did make a more calm, quiet, innocent recreation than angling, nor, it may be well added, worthier types of the good virtues of the angler than themselves. May they long continue to enjoy the savory shad upon the smoking board, the crisp, white catfish, and the steaming rock, "dishes of meat too good for any but anglers, or very honest men."

---

[1] The Fairmount Dam.
[2] In 1745 there were but 2049 houses in Philadelphia; in 1871, 122,751.

THE ZOOLOGICAL GARDEN.

The entire tract, embracing "The Solitude," the grounds of the old Fishing-House, and an estate formerly known as Spring Hill, was transferred by a lease from the Park Commissioners to the Zoological Society of Philadelphia. It covers thirty-three acres; its boundaries are the River Road and the Pennsylvania Railroad, Thirty-fifth Street and Girard Avenue. The Garden has every variety of surface; it has a piece of old woodland — the Solitude Grove, large water supply, and the most complete drainage. The Solitude Villa — the former residence of John Penn, has been restored and preserves an interesting association of the grounds. The improvements are of a very ornate, as well as durable, character. The collection of Birds and Animals is already large, and constantly increasing by the private agencies of the Society, donations, and contributions from officers and others in the army and naval service, made by permission of the Government of the United States.

The Society was incorporated March, 21, 1859. The Garden was first opened July 1, 1874. It is open for visitors every day during the entire year. A moderate charge for admission is made.

OFFICERS.

President.
WILLIAM CAMAC, M. D.

Vice-Presidents.
J. GILLINGHAM FELL.   GEORGE W. CHILDS.

Corresponding Secretary.
JOHN L. LECONTE, M. D.

Recording Secretary.
JOHN SAMUEL.

Treasurer.
FRANK H. CLARK.

Actuary,
CHARLES L. JEFFERSON.

Managers.

William S. Vaux,   S. Fisher Corlies,
Frederick Graff,   Theodore L. Harrison,
William Hacker,   Henry C. Gibson,
J. Vaughan Merrick,   Isaac J. Wistar,
John Wagner,   Edward Biddle,
William H. Merrick,   Charles W. Trotter.

GENERAL VIEW OF EXHIBITION GROUNDS.

THE EXHIBITION GROUNDS.

The visitor leaving the Garden may either continue on Girard Avenue to Elm Avenue, or under the Railroad Bridge.[1] By the latter he passes over Eaglesfield, a knoll of land partly covered by a wood, over which the road rises and descends to a bridge, then winds around a second knoll, passing over grounds formerly known as Peterstone; these contain

[1] The Pennsylvania Railway, connecting lines throughout the United States.

Sweet Briar Mansion;[2] passing again by a wood, the visitor enters the Exhibition Grounds.

These grounds were formally transferred by the Park Commissioners to the Commissioners of the International Exhibition on the 4th day of July 1873; and the Proclamation of the Exhibition made by order of the President of the United States. The reservation contains 450 acres; it extends from this point to George's Hill and Ridgeland, embracing two tracts—Landsdowne and Belmont; the first—Lansdowne, is bounded by the river, Elm Avenue — the Park's southern boundary, George's Hill, and the Belmont tract. It is a plateau known as the Lansdowne Plateau, and a second plateau lying north and westward — Lansdowne Terrace, separated by a ravine from the other. This first tract is the site of the National Memorial, the Main Exhibition Building, Agricultural and Machinery Halls, and the Horticultural Hall and grounds. Belmont, the second of these tracts, is bounded by the Lansdowne tract, Ridgeland, Elm Avenue, and the River; it is the reservation for Agriculture.

[2] Erected 1791, by John Ross, a merchant of Philadelphia; formerly the residence of Samuel Breck. See page 113.

THE MAIN EXHIBITION BUILDING

Is located on the Plateau east of Belmont and north of Elm Avenues. It stands 170 feet back from the north side of Elm Avenue, and 300 feet from the south side or front of the Art Gallery.

The building is in the form of a parallelogram, extending east and west 1,880 feet, and north and south 464 feet.

The larger portion of the structure is one story in height, and shows the main cornice on the outside 45 feet above the ground. At the centre of the longer sides of the building are projections 416 feet in length, and in the centre of the shorter sides or ends are projections 216 feet in length. In these projections are located the main entrances, which are provided with arcades upon the ground floor, and central facades extending to the height of 90 feet.

The East Entrance forms the principal approach for carriages.

The South Entrance for street-cars; the ticket-offices being located upon the line of Elm Avenue, with covered ways provided for entrance into the building itself.

The North Entrance communicates directly with the Art Gallery.

The West entrance gives the main passage-way to the Machinery Hall.

Upon the corners of the building are four towers 75 feet in height, and between the towers and the central projections or entrances, a lower roof, showing a cornice 24 feet above the ground.

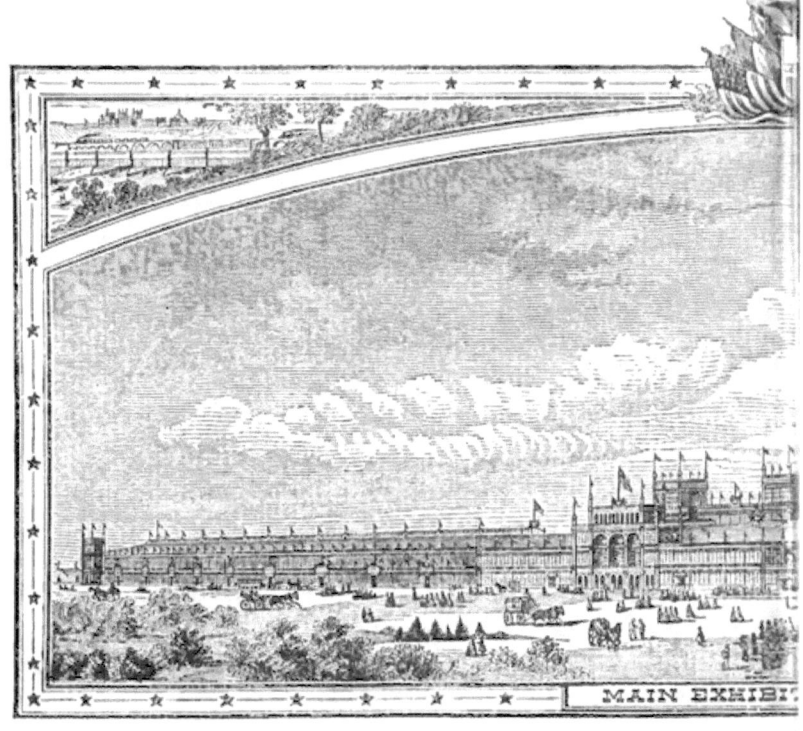

DIMENSIONS.

Measurements taken from centre to centre of supporting columns.

Length of Building	1880 feet.
Width of Building	464 "
CENTRAL AVENUE or NAVE.	
Length	1832 "
Width	120 "

FAIRMOUNT PARK.

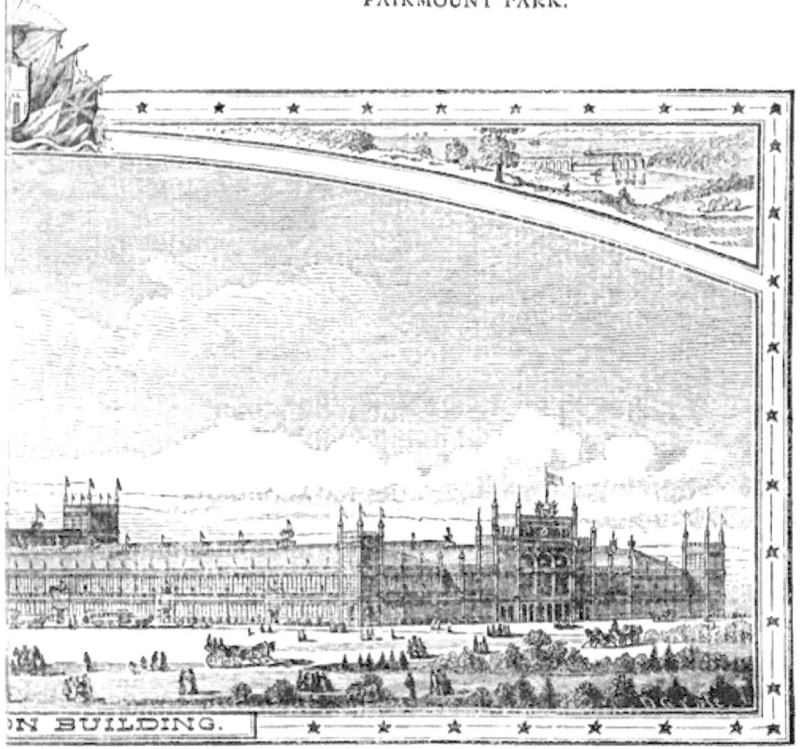

Height to top of supporting columns	45 feet.
Height to ridge of roof	70 "

CENTRAL TRANSEPT.
Length	416 "
Width	120 "
Height to top of columns	45 "
Height to ridge of roof	65 "

SIDE AVENUES.
  Length . . . . 1832 feet.
  Width . . . . 100 "
  Height to top of columns . . . . 45 "
  Height to ridge of roof . . . . 65 "

SIDE TRANSEPTS.
  Length . . . . 416 "
  Width . . . . 100 "
  Height to top of columns . . . . 45 "
  Height to ridge of roof . . . . 65 "

CENTRAL AISLES.
  Length at east-end . . . . 744 feet
  " at west-end . . . . 672 "
  Width . . . . 48 "
  Height to roof . . . . 30 "

SIDE AISLES.
  Length at east-end . . . . 744 "
  " at west-end . . . . 672 "
  Width . . . . 24 "
  Height to roof . . . . 24 "

CENTRAL SPACE or PAVILION.
  Ground Plan . . . . 120 " square.
  Height to top of supporting columns . . . . . 72 "
  Height to ridge of roof . . . . 96 "

TOWERS OVER COURTS.
  Ground Plan . . . . 48 " square.
  Height of Roof . . . . 120 "

CORNER TOWERS.
  Ground Plan . . . . 24 " square.
  Height to roof . . . . 75 "

The foundations consist of piers of masonry.

The superstructure, of wrought-iron columns and wrought-iron roof trusses.

The columns are placed lengthwise the building, at the distance of 24 feet apart; and the sides of the building, for the height of seven feet from the ground, are finished with timber framed in panels between the columns, and, above the seven feet, with glazed sash. Portions of the sash are movable for ventilation,

The wrought-iron columns are composed of rolled channel bars with plates riveted to the flanges.

The roof trusses are similar in form to those in general use for Depôts and Warehouses.

Upon the exterior of the building, around each corner column, is placed a light casing of galvanized iron, octagonal in form, and designed to appear as a slender turret extending from the ground to above the roof.

The roof over the central part, for 184 feet square, is raised above the surrounding portion, and four towers, 48 feet square, rise to 120 feet in height at the corners of the elevated roof.

The areas covered are as follows:

Ground Floor	872,320 square feet.	20.02 acres.
Upper Floors, in projections	37,344 " "	.85 "
" " in towers	26,344 " "	.60 "
	936,008	21.47

GROUND PLAN.

The Ground Plan shows a central avenue or nave 120 feet in width, and extending 1,832 feet in length. This is the longest avenue, of that width, ever introduced into an Exhibition Building. On either side of this nave is an avenue 100 feet, by 1,832 feet in length. Between the nave and side avenues are aisles 48 feet; and, on the outer sides of the building, smaller aisles 24 feet in width.

Three cross-avenues or transepts of the same widths, and in the same relative positions to each other as the nave and avenues, run lengthwise; viz.: a central transept 120 feet in width by 416 feet in length, with one on either side of 100 feet by 416 feet, and aisles between of 48 feet.

The intersections of these avenues and transepts in the central portion of the building result in dividing the ground floor into nine open spaces free from supporting columns — covering in the aggregate an area of 416 feet square. Four of these spaces are 100 feet square, four 100 feet by 120 feet, and the central space or pavilion 120 feet square. The intersections of the aisles result in four interior courts 48 feet square, one at each corner of the central space.

The main promenades through the nave and central transept, are each 30 feet in width, those through the centre of the side avenues and transepts 15 feet each. All others are 10 feet wide.

The Private Offices for the various Foreign and State Commissions are on the ground floor and in the second story on either side of the Main Entrances, in close proximity to their exhibited products.

Buffets or Restaurants for light refreshments are at four prominent points.

Water is supplied freely throughout the entire building, the most complete provision being made for protection against fire.

Sanitary arrangements, easy of access, are located at six different points.

ARRANGEMENT OF PRODUCTS.

The arrangement of products exhibited is that recommended by the Committee on Classification of, and adopted by, the U. S. Centennial Commission. It is known as the Dual System of Classification, and will be applied in this building as follows:

Dept. I.   Materials in their unwrought condition. Mineral, vegetable, and animal.
Dept. II.   Materials and Manufactures the result of extractive or combining processes.
Dept. III.   Textile and Felted Fabrics. Apparel, costumes, and ornaments for the person.
Dept. IV.   Furniture and Manufactures of general use in construction and in dwellings.
Dept. V.   Tools, Implements, Machines, and Processes.
Dept. VI.   Motors and Transportation.
Dept. VII.   Apparatus and Methods for the increase and diffusion of knowledge.
Dept. VIII. Engineering, Public Works, Architecture.
Dept. IX.   Plastic and Graphic Arts.
Dept. X.   Objects illustrating efforts for the improvement of the Physical, Intellectual, and Moral Condition of Man.

In this building will be located portions of all of the above Departments, except No. VI., which will be placed in the Machinery Hall, and No. IX. to which the Art Gallery will be especially devoted.

The Departments will be arranged in parallel zones lengthwise the Building, the zones being of different widths, according to the bulk of the products exhibited in the particular department. The countries and States exhibiting will be arranged in parallel zones crosswise the Building; these zones also being of different widths, according to the amount of space required for the exhibits of each country. Between each Department and each country will be passage-ways, distinctly marking the limit of each.

The result of this dual system will be, that any visitor or student desiring to compare products of the same kind from different parts of the world may do so by passing through the building lengthwise, keeping in the zone devoted to the particular Department; or desiring to examine the products exhibited by any particular Country or State may do so by passing through the Building crosswise, in the zone devoted to the particular Country or State.

GROUND PLAN AND ORIGINAL ALLOTMENT OF SPACE

	Square feet.	Sq. metres.
China	7,290	667
Japan	7,290	667
Liberia	2,268	210
Sandwich Is.	3,888	361
Hayti	3,888	361
Argent. Conf.	15,552	1,444
Brazil	17,520	1,627
Chili	9,744	905
Peru	11,664	1,083
U. S. Colomb.	7,778	722
Ecuador	3,888	361
Venezuela	5,508	521
Nicaragua	4,536	421
San Salvador	4,536	421
Guatemala	5,508	521
Honduras	3,888	361
Mexico	11,664	1,083
Orange		
Reserved space	17,520	1,627
U. S. America	123,832	11,404

IN THE MAIN EXHIBITION BUILDING.

	Sq. feet.	Sq. metres.
Great Britain,		
Canada,	46,610	4,328
India,		
Australia, and other Colonies,		
France, Algeria, and other Colonies,	27,264	2,531
Spain and Colonies,	15,552	1,444
Italy	11,664	1,083
Switzerland	6,158	572
Belgium	17,820	1,650
Netherlands, Denmark,	7,776	722
German Empire	27,264	2,531
Austria	23,328	2,100
Sweden, Norway,	10,044	947
Russia	10,044	947
Turkey	7,776	722
Egypt	7,776	722
Persia	7,776	722
Siam	3,948	367

The allotment is provisional and subject to modification to conform to the bulk of exhibits.[1]

From the Main Building a broad avenue extends westward to the Machinery Halls and a passage northward to the National Memorial, a structure now rapidly advancing to completion.

These three buildings are grouped together and made directly accessible by the Reading Railroad, the street lines of cars, by boats, and by the Pennsylvania Railroad, which passes up to the south fronts of the Main Exhibition Building and the Machinery Hall.

[1] The following changes have been made in the original allotment of space:—

France	will occupy	43,314.5 sq. ft.	Sweden	will occupy	15,358.8 sq. ft.
Switzerland	"	6,646.8 "	Norway	"	6,897 "
United States	"	166,351.7 "	Netherlands	"	8,167.5 "
England	"	51,776.3 "	Germany	"	27,975.5 "
Canada	"	24,070.8 "	Austria	"	24,070.8 "
Australasia, including India & other colonies	"	24,070.8 "	Japan	"	6,566.8 "
			China	"	7,504 "
			Denmark	"	5,647.5 "
Great Britain (total)	"	99,917.9 "	Orange	"	1,057.5 "
Spain	"	15,609 "	Sandwich Islands	"	1,462.5 "
Hungary	"	6,646.8 "	U. S. Colombia	"	2,337 "
Persia	"	2,015 "	Ecuador	"	2,432 "
Egypt	"	5,146 "	Venezuela	"	2,337 "
Siam	"	2,015 "	Arg. Confed.	"	2,432 "
Turkey	"	4,895.8 "	Hayti	"	2,128 "
Peru	"	40,518.8 "	Honduras Guatemala San Salvador	"	4,816 "
Chili	"	10,542.8 "			
Mexico	"	6,897 "			
Belgium	"	15,358.8 "	Brazil		6,897 "

ALLOTMENT TO OCT. 1, 1875.
HENRY PETTIT.

GEORGE'S HILL.

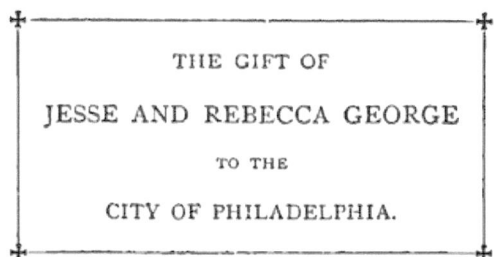

THE GIFT OF
JESSE AND REBECCA GEORGE
TO THE
CITY OF PHILADELPHIA.

The view from this concourse is a very commanding one. The background is shut in by a wood; but looking southward and westward, the hill descends gradually and widens to a broad open reach of greensward with trees—in clumps, separate, and in pieces of woodland—the remains of the primeval forests. Farther on, in the middle-ground of this fair landscape, ribboned through with floating lines of vapor from passing trains, flows the clear, broad Schuylkill—spanned with its bridges, dotted with pleasure steamers and the gay pennons of the navy barges. Beyond are wooded slopes and green open spaces; from them the eye wanders over the city's long-extending streets, spires, and domes, amid which rise in pure whiteness the pillars of the College. Farther yet, beyond these spires, these domes, these pillars, the eye defines the city's boundaries and the horizon's verge, and along this line, in a clear atmosphere, the sails of vessels on the river Delaware.

On fine afternoons this Hill is the grand centre for carriages; the whole summit is crowned with equestrians and pedestrians, carriages, rich dresses and gay liveries. The animation of the scene, heightened by inspiriting strains of music, by the sense of health and enjoyment which breathes about the place, and, most of all, by its grateful memory, renders it to visitors one of the most attractive portions of the Park.[1]

THE BELMONT RESERVOIR

adjoins George's Hill. It is supplied from the Belmont Works, on the margin of the river below. Its capacity is 35,800,000 gallons. The water-level, when full, is two hundred and twelve feet above the city datum. The arrangement by which the water passes from the main pipe into the basin is quite novel, and repays the short walk over from the Hill. There is also a very fine view from its east side of the city, and surrounding Park grounds on both sides of the river.

From George's Hill, the main carriage road leaves the reservoir on the right, and passes over a high plateau to Belmont.

[1] See page 128.

MACHINERY HALL

is located at a distance of 542 feet from the west front of the Main Exhibition Building, and 274 feet from the north side of Elm Avenue. The north fronts of the two buildings are on the same line, thus presenting from the east to the west ends of the Exhibition Buildings a frontage of 3824 feet on the principal avenue within the grounds.

The Hall is 360 feet wide by 1402 feet long, with an annex on the south side for hydraulic machines 208 feet by 210 feet. The entire area covered by the Main Hall and annex is 558,440 square feet, or 12.82 acres, giving, as arranged, 14 acres of floor space in the building.

The structure is one story in height, showing the main cornice 40 feet, and the ventilators 70 feet from the ground. The long lines of the exterior are broken by projections on the four sides; the main entrances are finished with façades, extending 78 feet in height. The east entrance is the principal entrance for visitors by the street-cars, from the Main Exhibition Building, and the Pennsylvania Railroad.

The foundations consist of piers of masonry. The superstructure consists of outer walls, solid timber columns supporting roof trusses, constructed with straight wooden principals and wrought iron ties and struts. The outer walls are built of masonry to a height of 5 feet, and above that are composed of glazed sash placed between the columns, and movable for ventilation. The columns are 16 feet apart, and placed lengthwise of the building. They are 40 feet high, and sustain the roof trusses over the avenues; the roof trusses are respectively 90 and 60 feet spans. Louvre ventilators are introduced in continuous lengths over both the avenues and the aisles.

The shafting consists of eight main lines, extending nearly the entire

FAIRMOUNT PARK.

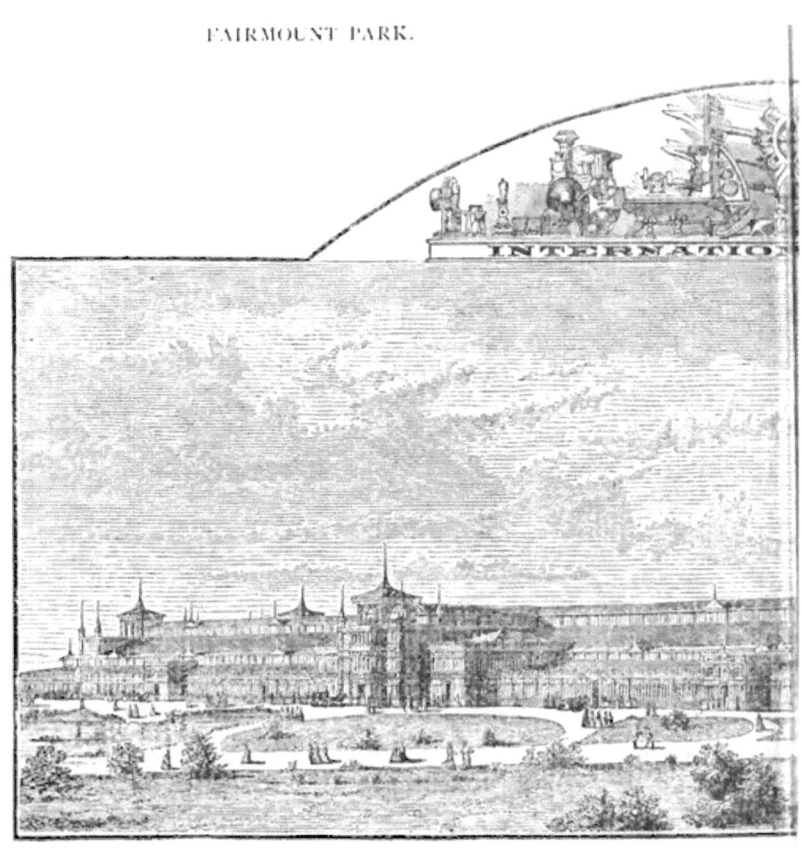

MACHINE

Extreme length . . . . 1402 feet
  " width . . . . 360 "
Annex 208 x 210 feet.

FAIRMOUNT PARK.

HALL.

Height of main cornice . . . . 40 feet.
Area of Hall and Annex 558,440 square feet.
Entire floor space 14 acres.

length of the structure, with counter-shafts introduced at points along the aisles. The hangers will be attached to the wooden horizontal ties of roof trusses, or to brackets especially designed for the purpose, projecting from the columns.

The boiler houses are along the south side of the Hall. The annex for hydraulic machines contains a tank 60 by 160 feet, with depth of water of 10 feet.

A central and four other avenues extend lengthwise the building, each 1360 feet long; these are crossed by a central transept, and four other avenues on either side; the central transept is 208 feet long, extending into the annex. The two avenues on either side of the central avenue and the central transept are each 90 feet wide; the others are each 60 feet. The promenades in the avenues on either side the central are 15 feet in width; in the central transept 25 feet, and in the other avenues 10 feet; exit doors are provided at the ends of the avenues.

THE HORTICULTURAL EXHIBITS.

A large portion of the exhibits of this Department will be arranged on the ground lying between this building and the building for the Conservatory; avenues for the proper display of these are being laid out through them. The principal of these is called Fountain avenue, extending from the Centennial Fountain—shown on the drawing—to the Conservatory, and will afford along its entire length an effective view of the large and varied exhibits of this Department; the fountain itself, embracing five colossal figures, will be a grand object on the grounds.

THE NATIONAL MEMORIAL.

ART GALLERY.

This structure — one of the affixes to the Exhibition, is located on a line parallel with, and three hundred feet northward of, the Main Building.

It is on the most commanding portion of the Lansdowne Plateau, and is elevated on a terrace six feet above its general level.

The materials are granite, glass, and iron. The structure is 365 feet in length, 210 feet in width, and 59 feet in height, over a spacious basement 12 feet in height.

The Main Front looks southward; it displays three distinctive features: A Main Entrance in the central section; a Pavilion at each end; and two Arcades connecting the Pavilions with the centre. The Central Section is

95 feet long, 72 feet high; Pavilions, 45 feet long, 60 feet high; Arcades, each, 90 feet long, 40 feet high.

The front, or south face of the Central Section, displays a rise of thirteen steps to the entrance 70 feet wide. The entrance is by three arched doorways, each 40 feet high and 15 feet wide, opening into a hall. Between the arches of the door-ways are clusters of columns terminating in emblematic designs.

The doors are relieved by bronze panels, having the coats-of-arms of all the States and Territories.

In the centre of the main frieze is the United States coat-of-arms.

The main cornice is surmounted by a balustrade with candelabras. At either end is an allegorical figure.

A dome rises from the centre of the structure to the height of 150 feet from the ground. It is of glass and iron: from it a colossal figure rises.

Groups, also of colossal size, stand at each corner of the base of the dome.

The pavilions display windows 30 feet high and 12 feet wide.

The arcades are intended to screen the long walls of the gallery. Each consists of five groined arches, looking outward over the grounds and interiorily over open gardens, which extend back to the main wall of the building.

The gardens are 90 feet long and 36 feet deep, ornamented in the centre with fountains and designed for the display of statuary. From them stairways reach the upper line of the arcades which forms promenades 35 feet above the ground.

The balustrade is ornamented with vases, and is designed ultimately for statues.

The cornices, the atticas, and the crestings throughout, are highly ornamented.

THE AGRICULTURAL BUILDING

Stands north of the Horticultural Building, and east of Belmont Avenue. The extreme dimensions of the building are 540 feet in front, by 800 feet in depth, consisting of a central nave 800 in depth, by 100 feet in width, with a central transept 100 feet in width by 540 feet in depth, and two side transepts 80 feet in width by 540 feet in depth. The nave and transept section are constructed of Howe trusses, built curvilinearly, and set to the form of two sides of an equilateral Gothic arch, springing from the ground line. The principals are set to uniform spacings of 20 feet between centres, the depth of truss being 4 feet 6 inches for the 100 feet span, and 3 feet 9 inches for the 80 feet spans.

At the intersection of the nave and central transept the diagonal trusses are coupled, separated 8 feet by lattice bracing, converging from 10 feet in depth at the foot to 6 feet at the base of dome and lantern. The intersection of 80 feet transepts with the nave are proportionately less, but of similar construction.

The intervening areas between the nave and transept sections are inclosed by shedding.

The entire structure is of timber left from the saw, finished upon interior surfaces by alum-sized color wash.

The exterior siding and frontal lines are planed for painting.

The section of building formed by the arch trusses receives light direct —by glass sections in planes forming roof cover—their stilt at the base constructed as louvres for ventilation.

The descriptions of the several buildings have been prepared from specifications and notes furnished by the architects and engineers to the author.

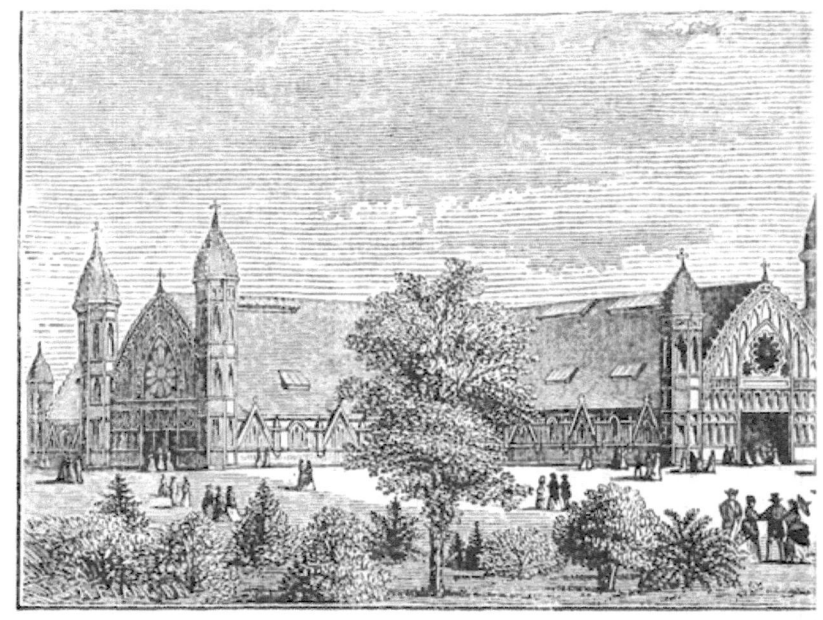

THE AGRICULT

The intervening shedding has lantern lights continuous through their depth, in each bay of 60 feet.

The truss system adopted for the major portion of the building provides roof and wall construction, in the one element a truss, and incloses the extended floor area in the simplest manner; the elevation of the roof section converging to the ridge lessens the effect of the sun's heat, to which with-

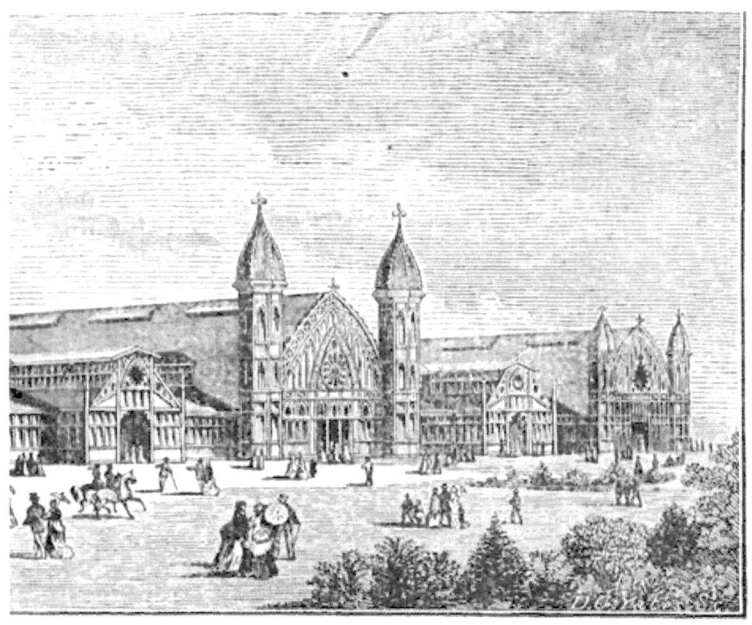

BUILDING.

out the protection of a ceiling beneath, a building inclosed by temporary roof cover would be subject in the summer season.

An object of the structure is economy of space, and in this view simplicity of construction has been sought, rather than embellishment.

The building is drained by sewage beneath the floor. The Architect is JAS. H. WINDRIM; Contractor, PHILIP QUIGLEY.

THE BUILDING FOR UNITED STATES EXHIBITS

Occupies ground north of the Machinery Hall, and west of Belmont Avenue. Its front width is 340 feet, depth 480 feet; it consists of a central nave 60 feet by 480 feet; a cross transept 60 feet by 340 feet, with aisle and annex section covering a floor area 102,840 square feet.

The centre of each façade has a principal entrance, the architecture of which will relieve the simplicity of the shed construction of the general building.

It is well lighted and ventilated, and provided with water stations distributed through the building; it is built of timber, the exterior faces only being painted. Architect, JAS. H. WINDRIM; Contractor, AARON DOANE.

THE JURY PAVILION

Stands in the rear, at the distance of 150 feet from the Main Exhibition and Machinery Buildings. It is 152 feet long and 115 feet wide, two stories, with 4 towers. It consists of a main hall, on the first floor, 60 x 80 feet, 43 feet high, and an adjoining hall 25 x 60 feet, 25 feet high, separated by removable partitions; a corridor 10 feet wide extends around the main hall, opening on committee rooms; on this floor, also, are four rooms for offices; the second floor is composed of a gallery around the main hall, and a third hall 22 x 60 feet, for committees; the material is wood. Architect, H. J. SCHWARZMANN; Contractor, LEVI KODER.

GOVERNME

BUILDING.

THE HORTICULTURAL BUILDING

Is located on the Lansdowne Terrace, northward of and separated by Lansdowne Ravine from the National Memorial. It occupies the site of a mansion formerly the residence of John Penn,[1] the last colonial governor of Pennsylvania. The design is the Moresque style of the twelfth century; the principal materials are iron and glass. The length of the building is 383 feet, its width 193 feet, and extreme height 72 feet.

The main floor is occupied by the central conservatory, 230 by 80 feet, and 55 feet high, surmounted by a lantern 170 feet long, 20 feet wide, and 14 feet high. There are two hot-houses on the north, and two

[1] See page 118.

on the south side of the conservatory; each of these is 100 by 30 feet. On the east and west sides of the conservatory are restaurants. Architect, H. J. SCHWARZMANN, who is also the architect of the National Memorial; Contractor, JOHN RICE. The Memorial works being executed abroad and here, and to be placed on the grounds, are advancing to completion. Among these are the Humboldt Monument, the African Sibyl for the Woman's Department; the Centennial C. T. A. of America Fountain, the Columbus and Witherspoon Monuments, and the Hebrew Monument—the Statue of Religious Liberty, designed for the national ceremonies July 4, 1876.

THE BUILDING FOR THE WOMAN'S DEPARTMENT,

Situated near the Main Exhibition Building, is a structure covering 30,000 square feet; it exhibits a nave and transept each 192 feet long, and 64 feet wide, terminating in porches 8 x 32 feet. Four pavilions, each 48 feet square, occupy the angles formed by the nave and transept. The centre of the structure rises 25 feet above the exterior portions, and terminates with a cupola and lantern, 90 feet from the ground; the entire superstructure rests on the exterior walls and four supporting columns; the material is wood roofed over by segmental trusses. It contains, in addition to space for exhibits, toilet and reception rooms. Architect, H. J. SCHWARZMANN; Contractors, JONES & LEWIS. In addition to these buildings are buildings for separate exhibits, and the buildings for the several States and foreign Commissions.

BELMONT.

JUDGE PETERS'S FARM.

On this place, twenty-five years ago, was still standing what Downing describes as the grandest avenue of hemlocks in America. These trees were centenarians in the perfection of their growth, ninety feet high, some draped with immense masses of English ivy. This long and stately avenue extended from the mansion to a road beyond the Belmont Avenue, and was there terminated by an obelisk. Many of these hemlocks yet remain. The garden walks were finished with box and privet, the beds set with rare shrubs and flowers, and the grounds adorned with vases and statues. The mansion, which is described by Chastellux (1780) as "a tasty little box, in the most charming spot nature could embellish," remains with little alteration, and is a very excellent specimen of the houses of that early period. Its principal characteristics are a broad hall and small dormitories, small window-glass and heavy sashes, highly ornamented and high wooden mantel-pieces, a comfortable dining-room, and open fireplaces. One of these in the hall is still used; the panel over it formerly held a landscape; the coat of arms of the family remains perfect on the ceiling. Other ornamental devices about the mansion are recognizable as belonging to that early period. The roof has been raised; the third story and piazza are modern. A library, which adjoined the main house, has also been removed since the Judge's time. The date of the erection of the main out-building is fixed by a monogram, T. W. P. 1745, cut on a slab set in the wall. There was a chestnut-tree near this mansion, planted by Washington, known as the Washington tree,[1] and an object of great interest in former times. There is still standing there a white walnut, which was planted by Lafayette, on his visit here as the nation's guest, in 1824.

[1] Washington and Judge Peters proposed walking one afternoon. When a few steps from the back hall-door of the mansion, the Judge handed the General a large chestnut (a Spanish nut). Washington suggested planting it; thereupon the Judge, who carried a cane (Washington never carried a cane), made a hole with it in the ground, Washington dropped the nut, the Judge earthed it over. The shoot from it was watched and tended with care; it grew to be a large tree, and bore nuts of extraordinary size. This tree stood on the right hand, a few steps outside the hall-door. The two trees near the dining-room are its lineal descendants.

See page 120.

MOUNT PROSPECT.

This portion of the Park,[1] unlike the rest, has no legendary or historic associations; but it requires none—as a natural throne, it asserts the authority of its position.

In one field of view, it embraces the most distant sections of the city, widely separated villages, and still more widely separated ranges of country.

The Schuylkill lies under its mountain-like side, here a lake and there a winding river. The Park, in its whole extent to Fairmount, spreads map-like beneath it. The waters of the far Delaware show from it, mile after mile, on their long journey to the sea. Beyond, pine forests stretch away in the dim distance, and hang a dark fringe along the horizon.

From the mansion[1] extends a grand panorama; for its background, rocky ranges, deep glens, and dark woodlands, villages, and farm-lands; and for its foreground, all the broad acres of this pleasure-ground, the spires and domes of the second city of the continent, and the great rivers which are its wealth and life-giving boundaries.

Mount Prospect has yet more to offer than this panorama; as if to leave nothing wanting in which it should challenge supremacy, on its summit, the one beside the other, stand three forest-trees, larger and more impressive than any others through the whole Park limits; one of these trees is a Black Walnut, another a Chestnut, the third a Tulip Poplar.

These giant old trees, the relics and remembrancers of "the times which tried men's souls," stand there, nature's noblemen, granting favors and asking none.

They have suggested the famous meeting of the three allied sovereigns in Hyde Park.[2] But may they not better suggest the enduring companionship of three other and nobler sovereigns—the Black Walnut, with its rich solid wood, Morris; the Chestnut, with its broad, liberal branches, Jefferson; the Tulip Poplar, the noblest of all the forest-trees of America, Washington—the purse, the charter, and the sword of the Revolution; men who loved these grounds, strong men who stood together, in their

---

[1] Built in 1802 by George Plumstead, a merchant of Philadelphia engaged in the India trade.

[2] After Napoleon's fall.

day and generation, as these trees stand, changeless and mighty, in sunshine and in storm.

> " . . . THE GREAT OF EARTH,
> GREAT NOT BY KINGLY BIRTH,
> GREAT IN THEIR WELL PROVED WORTH—
> FIRM HEARTS, AND TRUE."

THE EAST BANK.

This section of the Park will be opened to the public this summer. A proposed road will make it accessible from Fairmount by a continuation of the present river road on the east bank, which will turn to the right after passing through the tunnel.

The section is a series of estates—among others, Fountain Green, Mount Pleasant, Rockland, Belleville, Ormiston, Edgeley, Woodford, and the Strawberry Mansion; they lie in successive tracts along the river, beginning below the Columbia Bridge and terminating at Laurel Hill. Its principal advantages over the west bank are more commanding views of the river and a more absolutely natural condition. The thickets remain, and a greater wealth of flowers in the woods and valleys. There is not an inch of frightful smoothness in the whole distance along the river bluff from the present entrance at Columbia Bridge to the Cemeteries. Among the many attractions of this section of the Park there are three: the first, a grand ravine; the second, the splendid trees on the Rockland estate; and the third, a broad view of the river, which, once seen, will never be forgotten by any true lover of nature; nor should such a one fail to find the young tree which stands, like a tower solidly set on a rock, in that ravine, or the gnarled chestnut, near Laurel Hill. This section[1] contains two mansions of historic importance. The Woodford Mansion, situated on the Ridge Avenue, was built by William Coleman,[2] the friend of Franklin. It was afterwards the residence of David Franks, a gentleman with large business connections in Philadelphia and New York during and after the Revolution. His son, Major Franks, was aid-de-camp to Arnold before his defection, but was himself a true patriot. His daughter, Miss Franks,[3] was celebrated for her wit and beauty in the days of the republican court. It was also afterwards the residence of William Lewis, one of the most distinguished among the advocates of Philadelphia.

The other of these mansions overlooks the river near the Columbia Bridge.

---

[1] The lake reservoir to be located in this section will be one hundred and six acres in extent, with ninety acres of water surface, and will hold 750,000,000 gallons.

[2] Erected 1742.

[3] Miss Franks deserves to be remembered for her determined defences of her sister belles. In one of her letters she even says: "The ladies of Philadelphia have more cleverness in a turn of the eye, than the New York ladies in their whole composition."

MOUNT PLEASANT.

The stately mansion on this estate was built by John Macpherson, who was its owner from 1761 to 1779. William Macpherson, his son, was born in Philadelphia in 1756. He was at thirteen a cadet in the British army. While adjutant of the 16th Regiment in Florida, he tendered his resignation. On his return to New York, he obtained permission from Sir Henry Clinton to resign, declaring he would never serve against his countrymen. He joined the Continental army on the Hudson in 1779; was made a major by brevet, and stood high in the confidence of Washington. He is famous as the organizer and commander of Macpherson's blues in the insurrection of 1794, and served under General Mifflin.

The mansion passed from John Macpherson to Benedict Arnold

(March, 1779), and through him, immediately afterwards, to trustees, as a marriage settlement for Mrs. Arnold, reserving to himself a life-estate. His defection took place the following year. It was followed by the forfeiture of his life-interest. The mansion then became the residence of General Von Steuben, known with us as the Baron Steuben. Of late years it has been the scene of many of those grand celebrations which distinguish the German Fatherland.

Baron Steuben, whose residence here associates his name with this mansion, was a life-long soldier.

As a boy, witnessing the Siege of Prague; as a youth, serving through the Seven Years' War, a member of the personal staff of Frederick the Great. He came here a veteran from his strict school, and encouraged by that great King's sympathies with the cause of the Colonies. It is his enduring remembrance that he created the discipline of the American Army, and his alone.

Unambitious of fame, he retired after the close of the war, and in the far wilderness, near Trenton Falls, lived and died. At his own request, he was buried there; desiring only that he should be wrapped in his military cloak, and that the then unbroken silence of his burial-place should so remain. His name very honorably associates itself, on these grounds, with the many better remembered, but yet no more deserving of remembrance than this veteran disciplinarian. Through him the irregular bands of the Colonies became the armies of the Revolution.

THE RAVINES.

The ravines in the Park on the west side of the river are consecutively named the "Sweet Brier," the "Lansdowne," and the "Belmont" ravines, and Belmont Glen.

In these ravines, nature has been left to her own better hands. There are no close-shaven, sloping mounds of greensward, no formal groups of flowers, nor any exotic set out orderly to be the unnatural companion of the sturdy survivors of the old forest. The result is, that these ravines

are the most attractive places in the Park to real earnest lovers of nature
"Unkempt and wild, she reigns alone."

They may be visited separately by leaving the carriage and joining at the opposite side of the ravine, as can be very conveniently done at Lansdowne. But for the whole tour, a most healthful and enjoyable one, set out leisurely with a good pair of shoes and a quiet conscience, from the Lansdowne entrance. The bridle-path from this point keeps between the carriage road and the river for some distance, giving fine views. It joins the carriage road again at the railway bridge, but soon leaves it and passes in front of the mansion, entering there the first of these ravines.

SWEET BRIER RAVINE.

This ravine is attractive all the year round. It has a brook crossed by a bridge—

> "A hidden brook
> In the leafy month of June,
> That to the sleeping woods all night
> Singeth a quiet tune."

The path descends to the bridge and rises from it by rustic steps, all in excellent keeping with the character of the way. On every side are wild flowers, shrubs, and large forest-trees, many covered with hanging vines.

The path and road come out together at "the river road bridge."

From this point it soon winds again, seeks the shade of the forest-trees nearer the river, passes under them through thickets of undergrowth, and so descends gradually to

THE LANSDOWNE RAVINE.

Large forest-trees stand in this ravine, without any order. Some in friendly groups, some in separate dignities; some rise from the bottom of the ravine, some start boldly out from its steep sides; all in a very irregular but not the less most unimprovable manner.

A brook begins its little journey from a spring at the head of the ravine,[1] in some places hides itself under sprays of ferns, in others trickles and drops down broken ledges, and makes tiny mirrors over smooth-worn stones; all along its way hang drooping vines. It is a very unpretentious little brook, but, to eyes that see clearly, it is very attractive.

Crossing this brook, the path, by a miniature Alpine zigzag with rustic seats, reaches the Lansdowne concourse.

Leaving the concourse, it passes along the lawn, giving a broad view of the river on the right hand and the Lansdowne tract on the left, and so enters

THE BELMONT VALLEY.

The path here turns at a point which gives a view of the river looking northward, and ascends a bluff close to a precipice formed by a quarry, and descends along the side of the ravine.

The whole character of this ravine is wild and tangled with vines, ferns, trees, and wild flowers. It is a charming retreat for a summer morning or afternoon with books and leisure.

Leaving the ravine, the path joins the main carriage way, and another path on the opposite side continues on towards George's Hill and Belmont.

---

[1] There is a fine grove of the Angelica or Hercules club at the head of this ravine.

At Belmont, opposite the front of the mansion a guide board indicates a path to the river through

BELMONT GLEN.

This path is the most frequented in the Park; it descends by an easy grade to the Belmont Station on the Reading Railroad, and follows part of the way the course of a brook. It is shaded by forest-trees and vines, except where, in two places, it opens out for short distances to the sunlight, to which the grateful shadow quickly succeeds. The path crosses a rustic bridge half-way between the station and the mansion, and is good at all seasons.

There are, besides these, three other ravines on the west side of the river, one above Belmont, one near Mount Prospect, descending to the river, and the third at Mount Prospect, descending west. These have as yet no defined pathway. On the east bank of the river there is a very romantic ravine on the Fountain Green grounds, and the grand ravine which descends to the river near Ormiston.

All these ravines have springs of clear cold water.

THE RIVER ROAD.

In addition to the views afforded by the main carriage drive and the paths through the ravines, there is also a road along the river margin. This road shows points as interesting as the others. On the east bank it diverges from the main carriage road in the plaza at Fairmount, passes the boat-houses, and under the two bridges through an artificial tunnel, whence it will extend to the Falls and Wissahickon.

On the west bank it connects with the main carriage drive at the bridge beyond Sweet Brier, and there passing under this road, descends to the river, and comes out at the foot of Lansdowne Valley. It passes first

THE BELMONT WORKS.

These works supply the reservoir at George's Hill, and are operated by steam. Their pumping capacity is 10,000,000 gallons per twenty-four hours.

A SHORT distance beyond these works the road passes a low one-story cottage.

TOM MOORE'S COTTAGE.

"Alone by the Schuylkill, a wanderer, I strayed."

This cottage, with the two old trees, which in the lyric poet's time threw their grateful shadows over its low roof and humble door, are well stricken in years. The vine, which one of these trees has lifted into sunshine, still clings round it; but the old tree itself every spring-time buds forth more feebly its leaves, and will soon be gone. These fair Schuylkill banks were to Moore, as to others whose troubles were more real than those which ordinarily afflict the poet's over-sensitive existence, a "retreat so fair," as he has written—

"That his charmed soul forgot its wish to roam,
And rested there as in a dream of home."

He has left tributes of his genius to these scenes, and composed while among them[1] the sweetest of his ballads—

> "I knew by the smoke that so gracefully curled
> Across the green elms, that a cottage was near,
> And I said if there's peace to be found in this world,
> A heart that is humble might hope for it here."

It is a pleasant thing in this poet's memory, that these fair shores, then the abode of wild flowers and merry warblers, an undisturbed tranquillity of shade, should have been after so long a period, and after many rude invasions of trade, restored again to the natural condition in which he knew and loved them.[2]

After leaving the cottage, the road shaded by an avenue of trees extends for nearly a mile; it passes under the Railroad Bridge, and terminates at the Falls Bridge.[3]

---

[1] 1804.

[2] Celebrations in honor of Moore were formerly given in this cottage; of a characteristic one of these, there is a notice in the Press of June 11, 1858.

[3] The nearer of the bridges in the picture, on page 80, is the Railroad Bridge, the farther the Falls Bridge.

THE FALLS OF SCHUYLKILL.

The Falls, a name now applied to a village, was in former days the name of a natural cascade. A long rock projected from the foot of a hill at this point, and extended two-thirds the distance across the river, forming a dam. In the spring the water poured over it in a beautiful cascade; at other seasons it forced the river into a narrow channel, on the western side, with turbulence and great rapidity; the sound could be heard on still evenings a distance of several miles. The rock itself was characterized by singular indentations, caused probably by ages of attrition; among them was the apparent impression of a human foot, showing the heel, the hollow of the instep, the ball of the foot, and toes; it bore name the Devil's foot. It was believed to be an evidence of his real presence here. Time has made great changes in this place; factories have taken the place of fishermen's houses, paved streets of forest pathways, and the irregular and foam-bearded cascade, which gave the place its name, has yielded its inheritance to its smooth-faced younger brother, the steady-going mechanic at Fairmount. Tradition says this was the last place about Philadelphia deserted by the Indians. That it must have been much resorted to by them is proved by the fact that very numerous Indian relics have been and are still found here—stone axes, arrow-heads, and other instruments. As late as 1817 it was a famous fishing-place for shad,[1] perch, rock, and a migratory species of catfish, which came regularly about the 25th of May in numbers so numerous as to blacken the narrow passages of the river.[2] They were caught, upon the authority of eye-

[1] These were preserved by smoking, and were in great request in the winter. Our wise Founder did much belove them in this way, "Pray send us," he writes to his steward from Penn's Manor—"pray send us some two or three smoaked haunches of venizon; get them from the Swedes: also some smoaked shadds and beef—the old Priest at Philadelphia had *rare shadds*."

[2] This fish-story, unlike many others, is reliable, and within well-authenticated limits. Old John Holmes confirms it in this wise:—

> "We plenty have of many sorts of fish,
> As choice and good as any man could wish;
> Eels, rockfish, trout, shad, herring, perch, and pike,
> So plenty that I never saw the like."

The contests between the fishermen and the canoe-men, who traded on the river about 1722-32, were the subject of legislative action. The depositions of many canoe-men are in the archives of Pennsylvania (1732); among them, one Jonah Jones "Saith that in the month of February, it being extreme cold, he stroke fast on a fish-dam, and, to save his boat of wheat, was obliged to leap into ye river to ye middle of his body—afterwards proceeding with ye said wet clothes, they were frozen stiff on his back, by means whereof he underwent a great deal of misery." The first law passed by the State of Pennsylvania was an act to make this river navigable, and for the preservation of its fish.

witnesses, in nets often so full that the fishermen were unable to lift them into their boats. Shad were caught by dipping-nets; as many as could be raised by the hand were frequently taken at one time; a thousand of these fish have been taken there in those days in two sweeps of the seine. Of rockfish, from thirty to eighty pounds were taken during a morning. The hotels at this point were then the most popular places of resort[1] about the environs of Philadelphia, and are still much visited.

Back from the Falls, on an eminence on the east side of the Ridge Road, stands the former residence of Governor Mifflin. The house is a noticeable object in this vicinity.

THOMAS MIFFLIN.

Thomas Mifflin was a member of the Society of Friends. When the news of the battle of Lexington reached Philadelphia, he immediately assumed the cause of the Colonies. He was the youngest and most effective speaker who addressed the people on that occasion, and left immediately after for Boston, and there joined the army. Although his name has got mislaid among their records there, he yet, by his cool and

---

[1] Those ancient hotels, one of which was named in the old days Rock Fish Inn, still furnish regular meals—breakfast, dinner, and supper—having, except by special order, the same bill of fare as they served before the Revolution, and orderable always as "catfish and coffee." The bill of fare is catfish, beefsteak, broiled chicken, waffles, and coffee.

These catfish are, like their progenitors, a distinct fish from those which bear their name on the Delaware, and other rivers of this country; and, unlike them, are delicate in flavor and exceedingly good. These suppers are peculiar to Philadelphia. The fish are kept alive, winter and summer, in large covered boxes, through which fresh spring-water constantly runs.

intrepid conduct, much aided to establish the military reputation of that section of our country. He was engaged subsequently at the battle of Princeton, and his portrait is preserved in Trumbull's picture. He was the first Governor of Pennsylvania under the new constitution.

On the same side of the road, until a recent period, stood an octagon building once occupied as a school-house; its master was Joseph Neef, a pupil of Pestalozzi, of Switzerland.

JOSEPH NEEF.

"The Jolly old Pedagogue long ago."

For the school-children with whom once a year the city passes a day of unalloyed pleasure on these grounds, we wish to keep the memory green, of a man who taught school in this section of the Park, and in the octagon house.

He first brought school-children to the Park, and was himself all his life-long only one of these of larger growth.

And of all men who ever taught school, he was the best beloved by his scholars. He read the rules laid down by Solomon, backwards—spared the children and spoiled the rods. He built the Temple of Science at the foot of the hill, and made it as easy to get there as to coast on sleds in winter-time. He was out of doors with the boys all summer; never had a hat on his head nor a cent in his pocket; never got tired running up and down the hills; was the best swimmer and the best skater, and his boys the best swimmers and the best skaters in the whole neighborhood; he never had a book in his school, and could whistle through his fingers like a steam-whistle.

The old octagon house was full from the garret to the cellar of boys of all kinds, sizes, and dispositions, and everything was as pleasant in the school as if it had been "home in the holidays," and for many boys a great deal pleasanter. But what was best of all in that school, the smart boys grew smarter and the dull boys grew brighter, so that at last when a great prodigy[1] who had been born with his head full of figures, came there to puzzle them, they gave him harder puzzlers in return, and when he grew angry and struck out boldly with a switch which he carried, they doubled up hands and whipped him, and the old man laughed all the while. So here is to the memory of "the Jolly old Pedagogue" who first brought into this country the system of Pestalozzi[2] which revolutionized and humanized education, and the good influence of which is felt to this hour in all the common schools of America.

[1] Zerah Colborn.

[2] We are indebted to Mr. William McClure, the philosopher who endowed the Academy of Natural Sciences, for his sojourn and its good results here. He met him in Switzerland, and induced him to return with him to be his Master's Apostle in the New World.—*Hagner's Sketch of the Falls.*

FORT ST. DAVIDS.

Fort St. Davids was a rude but strong structure of heavy timber, cut from the opposite forests and erected long anterior to the Revolution. It was located at the foot of a hill, from which the rock forming the falls projected. On the hill a tall flagstaff was erected, from which floated King George's flag. In the interior hung a picture of his majesty and Queen Charlotte, and of Hendrick, King of the Mohawks. The room was decorated with an immense hat four feet in width, and other paraphernalia, dried fish, turtles, and Indian curiosities; a large bowl of "the great Mr. Pitt," wineglasses and decanters of curious workmanship, and a set of china with the Schuylkill arms. The company had also a flag on which were a moon, a fish, and a crown.

The Society of Fort St. Davids, the builders of this house and its gastronomic garrison, were companions of the Founder, and, like the former catfish of this stream, were accredited as a superior species; but, like those steadfast fishermen below, they had immense good times on all suitable occasions, and they never failed to make all unsuitable occasions suitable. They ultimately voyaged down the stream[1] to their brothers, then at the Baron Warner's, with whom they still dwell in indissoluble connection, capacious[2] both for good-humor and for fish. This garrison, during the Revolution, has a very noble record, in which good-humor was laid aside and its whole duty to the country sternly and fully done.

JOHN DICKINSON.

Among the names on the rolls of this Society is John Dickinson, the Author of "the Farmer's Letters."

This "shadow," rather than man, "slender as a reed, pale as ashes,"[3] this great writer, has been suffered to lapse almost into oblivion, yet it was in him God first lighted the fires of the Revolution. His letters made the cause of the Colonies heard before the throne of Great Britain, and it is his name only which is associated with Jefferson's as the writer

---

[1] Their house, in revenge for the part they took in the Revolution, was reduced to a heap of ruins by Hessian soldiers, who were quartered near Rock Fish Inn, under Gen. Kniphausen. They remained here some time after the Revolution, and rebuilt their house. The print represents the second house; it was destroyed by an accidental fire.

[2] Godfrey Schronk, a noted fisherman, assured John Watson, the chronicler, that the small garrison at Fort St. Davids cooked and put away often forty dozen catfish at a meal. At the house at Gray's Ferry, a notice of catches (1830) averages to one fisherman from five to twenty dozen white perch, and the aggregate catches, before their removal from the Baron Warner's, on fishing-days, ran fifty, eighty, and one hundred dozen.

[3] John Adams's description of Mr. Dickinson.

of the first official assertion of grievances which preceded the great Declaration. His words were the battle-cries of the Revolution. On these grounds they gave evidence of their power; although gentle blood ran in the veins of the peaceful inmates of Fort St. Davids, and their meats were set before them on heraldic plates, and the flag of English George floated over their house, yet Dickinson's words swept through its hewn logs like a storm; the flag went down—they answered his appeal with the sword. Here he might be fitly honored, as he was in his day and generation. The historic troop,[1] four of whose captains have been Governors of the State in Schuylkill, and the bar of Philadelphia, of which he was so worthy a representative, might unite and place on these grounds his monumental stone; and the words once written in his honor might well be graven there.

Pro Patria
John Dickinson
of the
City of Philadelphia.
The Author of the Farmer's Letters.
Ita cuique eveniat
Ut de Republica meruit.

---

[1] The First Troop Philadelphia City Cavalry.

LEAVING the Falls, and passing along the Ridge Road for the distance of three-quarters of a mile, we reach the mouth of the Wissahickon, marked by a high bridge, under which, crossing the stream, the road passes over

THE BATTLE GROUND.

The Ridge Road, from its intersection with Thirty-third Street to the south line of Laurel Hill, as also here, forms one of the boundaries of the portion of the Park lying on the east bank of the Schuylkill. Long before the Revolutionary War it was one of the principal roads leading from the city.

While the British under General Howe occupied Philadelphia, the surrounding country was open to their incursions through this road. To check them, Washington, from his camp at Valley Forge, ordered two thousand two hundred men, under the command of Lafayette, to make a sortie; and if, as then appeared probable, the British should evacuate the city, to hang upon and harass their rear-guard. Lafayette took a position at Barren Hill, on the Schuylkill, just above the upper boundary of the Park, and about ten miles from Washington's camp at Valley Forge. Howe determined to attack him without delay. On the morning of the 20th May, 1778, a detachment of five thousand men under General Grant, marching by a circuitous road, succeeded in turning Lafayette's left wing, and established itself nearly a mile in the rear of his position; another detachment, under General Gray, followed this road along the Schuylkill; the rest encamped at Chestnut Hill. These movements were discovered during the night by Captain McClane, a vigilant partisan officer, who hastened to the camp of Lafayette and apprised him of his danger. With great promptitude the General took the only course to preserve his detachment. With a few men he showed a head of column as though moving on Grant to attack him, while, by a rapid movement of the flank, his principal column crossed at Matson's Ford to the opposite bank of the river. Grant, finding them advantageously posted, did not choose to attack them; and his whole army returned to the city, having effected nothing. It was to this incident of the war that Lafayette alluded while partaking of the hospitalities of the ancient and honorable fishermen.

As a memento of the gratitude of the country for the services which he had rendered, Congress directed that a sword should be presented to him. It was prepared in France, under the supervision of Franklin. On the guard was engraved, among other memorable events in which Lafayette was distinguished by his prudence or his courage, "Retreat of Barren Hill." On transmitting the sword to Lafayette, Franklin addressed to him the following letter:—

TO THE MARQUIS OF LAFAYETTE.

PASSY, August 24, 1779.

SIR: The Congress, sensible of your merit towards the United States, but unable adequately to reward it, determined to present you with a sword as a small mark of their grateful acknowledgments. They directed it to be ornamented with suitable devices. Some of the principal actions of the war, in which you distinguished yourself by your bravery and conduct, are therefore represented upon it. These, with a few emblematic figures, all admirably well executed, make its principal value. By help of the exquisite artists France affords, I find it easy to express everything but the sense we have of your worth, and our obligations to you. I therefore only add, that, with the most perfect esteem, I have the honor to be, &c.

In this section of the Park also was fought a portion of the memorable Battle of Germantown; the British line of redoubts extended back of the Wissahickon Creek, along the east side, for a distance of two miles. During the battle the Americans occupied the hills, and until recently the remains of their temporary redoubts were visible, extending along the west side in a semicircle, a considerable distance.[1]

In building the Railroad Bridge which crosses here, these old landmarks were destroyed. A monumental shaft, at Roxborough,[2] commemorates some Virginia soldiers slain a short distance above this spot. Soldiers of other colonies moulder in the earth that lies between these sections of the Park.

[1] General Armstrong, the Commander of the Pennsylvania Militia, wrote to President Wharton (October 5, 1777), "We cannonaded from the heights on each side the Wissahickon, whilst the riflemen on opposite sides acted on the lower ground;" and, again, "One field-piece we got away, the other I was obliged to leave in the *horrenduous hills* of the Wissahickon."

[2] In the Leverington Cemetery.

THE WISSAHICKON.

This romantic stream, which still retains its Indian name,[1] lies between ranges of precipitous hills.

[1] Wisamickan, cat-fish creek; Wisaucksickan, yellow-colored stream.

Self-guarded by these rock battlements,[1] it retains that primeval character in which let us hope it will be always preserved. Along its banks through its whole extent, trees and vines hang down to the water's edge, and frequent springs drip from the rocks. Except at times in the spring and autumn when swollen with heavy rains, its waters have in many places scarcely a perceptible motion; it seems to be the bosom of a lake. Its unbroken quiet, its dense woodland, its pine-crowned hills, its sunless recesses, and sense of separation from the outer world, contrast strongly with the broad lawns, the open flowing river, and the bright sunshine which characterize the banks of the Schuylkill.

It is a chosen spot for youth and for old age, for all those whom simple love of nature contents; and it has been the home of romance, the theme of song, the source of illusions and of legends accredited in places not always obscure, from the earliest times to our own days.

---

[1] Until 1826 the Wissahickon was inaccessible except by by-roads and lanes. At the Ridge Road a mass of rock stood on one side and a precipice on the other. During that year the rock was removed, and the present road begun.

Until 1822 it emptied into the Schuylkill over a very picturesque fall of water, ten or twelve feet high.

Passing along the margin of the Wissahickon, the main carriage drive reaches first,

WISSAHICKON HALL.

At this saloon, which is a place of considerable resort, refreshments and ices are sold during the summer, and "catfish and coffee" at all seasons.

A short distance further on, the road passes a second restaurant,

THE MAPLE SPRING.

The restaurant which bears this name contains a collection of very grotesque figures of animals, birds, beasts, and serpents; these are all the uncut roots of the laurel, found in these forms in the earth. They are the labor of the proprietor's lifetime in the forests of this State.

Bateaux may be obtained at this restaurant, as also at the lower one, by the hour or for the afternoon or day, for excursions. The west bank of the stream at these points is most conveniently reached by this mode of conveyance.

THE HERMIT'S WELL

Is outside the Park limits; it is reached by crossing a bridge above Maple Spring, and passing along a lane which ascends through the woods. The well was dug by John Kelpius; the stonework yet remains. A venerable cedar, believed to have been planted by his hands, still throws its grateful shadows over it.

JOHN KELPIUS.

> "My food shall be of care and sorrow made,
>   My drink naught else but tears fallen from my eyes;
> And for my light in this obscure shade,
>   The flames may serve which from my heart arise;
> And at my gates despair shall linger still,
>   To let in death when love and fortune will."

Among the stories of the former dwellers in this romantic region, and of which reliable record remains, that of John Kelpius[1] holds a remarkable place. A scholar and a mystic, he came from Germany with his followers towards the close of the seventeenth century. They located themselves on this stream and dwelt in religious meditation, awaiting with anxious prayers the coming of the "Woman of the Wilderness."

Kelpius wore his young life away here, enduring to the end in patient expectation, fast and vigil, waiting morning and evening "the woman clothed with the sun, with the moon under her feet, and the twelve stars on her forehead; she who had fled into the wilderness."

---

[1] According to the Chronicon Ephratense, 1786, Kelpius was from Siebenburgen, and was of a wealthy family. He studied at Helmstadt under Dr. Fabricius, and was versed in the languages. His companions were all men in easy circumstances (freyen standes), and settled on the Ridge, which at that time was a wilderness, whence they named themselves "the woman in the wilderness." He died at the early age of thirty-five years, sitting in his garden, and attended by his followers weeping as for the loss of a father. The title of one of Kelpius's hymns reads: "Colloquium of the Soul with itself over her long during purification. Set in a pensive longing in the wilderness, Anno 1698, January 30."

Bartram, in 1761, makes this characteristic allusion to Dr. Witt, the favorite scholar of Kelpius, then eighty-three years of age: "Poor old man, he was lately in my garden, but could not distinguish a leaf from a flower." He was buried, at his own request, at the feet of Kelpius.

Some of his followers, who were afterwards known as the Hermits of the Ridge, fell away from the faith, others never woke from the strange delusion that brought them so long a journey. They also waited on in their caves among these rocks, with ever-renewing faith, the sign and visible presence, until, their weary limbs shrinking down and their eyes wearing out with watching, they died there, and the foxes made their burrows among their bones.

A QUARTER of a mile above the Log Cabin, and also on the opposite bank of the stream, a short distance above the bridge which crosses to the Hermits' Lane, is a high bluff; it is a striking object from the carriage road. The rock which rises from the bluff is called

THE LOVER'S LEAP.

The Lover's Leap overlooks from its crest a wild gorge. It is the scene of one of the numerous traditions which survive here. There is an illegible inscription in Latin, said to have been chiselled by Kelpius, on the face of the rock, and at various places around it aspiring Vandals have cut their initials. This rock stands two hundred feet above the surface of the stream.

FROM the rock a deep glen or gorge follows the stream.

THE HERMITS' GLEN.

This glen was a favorite spot with the hermits, the scene of their wanderings. It presents some of the most striking natural features along the stream. Immense boulders of many tons weight lie on the hill-sides; and a short distance above the "Lover's Leap," another rock juts out to the length of twenty feet. One feels, after climbing to the crest of this rock and looking far down upon the sharp stones in the gorge peering up through the holes and branches of undergrowing trees, not unlike the adventurer who crawls to the edge of Table Rock to look at Niagara.

FOLLOWING the main road a short distance further, a half mile in all above the Log Cabin, we reach a bend in the stream. Here it is joined by a creek coming down from the north; this creek, Paper-mill Run, is scarcely less picturesque in places than the Wissahickon. It joins the latter by a series of waterfalls. The lower of these has a perpendicular descent of about twenty feet over dark shale-like rocks. Near it stands the old house in which David Rittenhouse was born, and near its source the first paper-mill in America was erected by his ancestors in 1690.

DAVID RITTENHOUSE.

Kelpius had long gone to his rest, and Dr. Witt, his beloved scholar, almost blind with age and watching, was bending hopelessly over his grave, when David Rittenhouse raised his eyes also to the heavens, and with a stronger vision, by faith and by sight, penetrated their remote recesses.

David Rittenhouse, the astronomer, was of Holland ancestry; he followed first the plough, but was found so often with the plough lying in the furrow, and the fence full of figures, that he lost that service, and took up the trade of a clockmaker. His first great work, among many others—marvellous in their time, constructed wholly at night, his idle hours as he called them—was the famous orrery now in Princeton College. His next was a series of calculations for the transit of Venus over the sun's disk. This wonderful mechanical contrivance, the universe in motion on a frame, and these accurate and profound calculations, and their verification by his own observation, gave him a wide-spread reputation in this country and in Europe. The life of David Rittenhouse was mainly connected with the world of science, and his fame there rests; but, yet, his mind was also an invaluable machine for the business uses of his generation.

He was State Treasurer from 1777 to 1789, afterwards Director of the Mint, and for many years President of the Philosophical Society.

Of him Thomas Jefferson says: "We have supposed that Rittenhouse must be considered second to no astronomer living; as a genius first, because self-taught; as an artist, because he has exhibited as great a proof of mechanical skill as the world ever produced. He has not indeed made a world, but he has by imitation approached nearer his Maker than any mere man who has lived from the creation to these days." And this is further said, he gave no time to earn money beyond the most simple necessities of life, and although called to high offices, he had interest in them only as the performance of duties which were necessary for the well-being of his fellow-citizens. He lived—the first and most famous of that illustrious line through which America is rising to pre-eminence among the nations—a devotee of science; he died a sincere believer in the Christian revelation.

Beyond these points, the road reaches a bridge, over which it crosses to the opposite bank of the stream—the Red Bridge.

Beyond the bridge, half a mile further, on the opposite side of the stream, towers

MOM. RINKLE'S ROCK.

This is a precipice which begins at the stream's edge, and rises abruptly, a solid mass of rock, like a wall among the forest-trees. It has also its legendary story clinging around it; doled out around old firesides to credulous ears, while there were yet firesides and credulous natures.

That a poor old woman, as the story says, lived there, is very possible; that she fell from this giddy precipice, seems most probable; that she was a witch, drank dew from acorn cups, had the evil eye, and floated down the stream to the sea without sinking, is credible to witnesses only. Her name certainly survives, and adventurous boys, climbing this giddy height, shout it out to be called back to them from all the hills around, and so preserve it from generation to generation.

The rock, with the exception, perhaps, of Indian rock, is the grandest monarch of them all, and should have a name and association more appropriate than this legendary one. To ascend to its summit from the stream is difficult, and requires care; crossing the first bridge this side the monastery, turning immediately to the right, and keeping a woods-path, which in the spring has a continuous border of violets, you reach a steep hill-slope through which the rock rises—a friendly tree-branch here and there to grasp, a few minutes' rest after passing some piece of ground which slips the foothold, enables you with a little exertion to reach its summit. The rock juts out along its crest in an almost level ridge; it overlooks all the surrounding country; the lofty tops of the pine-trees show far below; yet further below, the dark recesses of the stream and the old monastery. All around, remote and near, is nature alone; city and town and busy haunts of men are all shut out by trees and hills and fields, the rock stands over all in solitude—and here, at sunset, when the always shadowy stream and dark pine-trees and deep recesses of the woods lie in a deeper shadow, this high rock stands lit with the golden light of the declining day, like a rich illumination on some missal's dark page—itself and all the scene a greater page of nature—an

> . . . "elder Scripture writ by God's own hand;
> Scripture authentic, uncorrupt by man."

A quarter of a mile further, two miles above the mouth of the stream, the road turns abruptly and continues on the same side, overhanging a precipitous chasm; another road at this point leaves the Park road, descends to and crosses the stream by a bridge; at the summit of the rise of the Park road, you see below: the bridge—a deep gorge—the stream abandoning its customary quiet, rolling, tumbling, and plashing over rocks—a mill in the gorge—and behind the mill a steep hill; on its summit stands an oblong stone building known for a century as

---

[1] This rock is on a tract of twelve acres, which skirt the stream, presented to the city by John Welsh.

THE MONASTERY.

Some of the windows of this building have been closed up, but the three encircling cornices above each story, the durable character of its masonry, the tall chimney, and a sort of venerable expression which looks out from its rough faces, indicate that it is a landmark of a past generation.

It was once used for a monastery. It stands upon high ground, but the tall ranges of hills tower high above it. A lane winds around the bend of the bluff and climbs up its steep side, forming in front of the house a semicircular lawn. In the valley below ("Willow Glen") there is a spot known as the Baptistery. Here the monks immersed their converts. The yard in the rear of the dwelling was used by them for the burial of their dead. Three steps of stone, rounded by the rains of years, lead to a sort of elevated plot encompassed by an old wall. Here the ritual was said, and the brothers chanted their burial-service. This building has stood there considerably over a century. Some accounts affirm that its inmates were of a Baptist order; others, which have a documentary attestation, that they were mystics, whose followers in manners and custom are still scattered along the region of Ephrata. Men certainly they were who came down close to nature, to the earth, and solitude, and sought out from the silence of desert places, however vainly, a pathway to THE LIGHT ILLIMITABLE.

The scenery at this point is very attractive. The suggestive old building; the trees along the hill-side set on rocks instead of natural soil; the road itself perched high above the chasm; the roaring and tumbling of the waters below as you ascend the hill; the change to silence as the carriage rolls along through a dense environing of forest-trees—are all impressive in a very remarkable degree.

A MILE further (three miles from the mouth of the Wissahickon), on the west bank, are certain caves, interesting to the antiquary.

THE CAVES.

The caves are situated in a lovely valley formed by the junction of a small stream with the Wissahickon. The most remarkable of them is referable to a certain period. It was excavated by miners led to the work by visions and witch-hazels indicating treasures there. Over it the rocks are about eighteen or twenty feet high, and much broken. Large forest-trees are growing on the summit. The cave or excavation extends into the solid rock thirty feet. It is five feet high, and five and a half wide; at the back part a man can stand erect. Fifty years after it had been closed, a venturous antiquary succeeded in getting under the huge root of a buttonwood which had grown across its mouth, and threaded its dark and narrow passages. He there witnessed the useless labors of the men in whose imaginations heaps of glittering gold had lain, luring them on to waste the best years of their lives, and, in a certain sense, to dig their own graves. The others of these caves are natural, have legendary histories traceable to no certain origins, perhaps holes for the bears and foxes, the resorts possibly of Indians; it may be Logan's wild Irish hound made in them his home.

A SHORT distance beyond (three and a half miles from its mouth), a bridge crosses the stream at one of the most striking pieces of landscape along this whole section of the Park. As you approach this bridge, on the opposite shore, in early spring, winter, and autumn, there is a strange effect of deciduous trees among evergreens; skeletons, as Doré would draw them, rising up along the verdure-crowned steep.

THE PIPE BRIDGE.

This bridge, finished last year, carries the water supply from the Roxborough to the Mount Airy reservoir at Germantown. It is a graceful structure, lifted a considerable height above the stream, and presenting the appearance of three light festoons hanging between the piers. The bridge is iron, and has four spans, each 172 feet 9 inches; its whole length is 691 feet, and it is supported by three iron piers, 83 feet high, set on masonry 20 feet high; an altitude of 103 feet above the level of the stream. Two twenty-inch water mains form the top cord of the bridge.[1]

---

[1] Dr. Franklin in his will (1780) recommends, " as a mark of his good-will, a token of his gratitude, and a desire to be useful to us after his departure," that a portion of the legacy left to accumulate for the benefit of the city of Philadelphia, be employed "at the end of one hundred years, if not done before, in bringing by pipes the water of the Wissahickon Creek into the town so as to supply the inhabitants." His legacy remains unused, but the work, by the appropriation of these creek borders and pipe connections, has now been completely done, and is a most appropriate tribute to his memory.

A HUNDRED yards above the Pipe Bridge, a wooden bridge crosses the stream; leaving the carriage and crossing this bridge, turning to the left and following a pathway a short distance along the hill-side, your progress will be arrested by a stream, Creshein Creek, which joins the Wissahickon. At this point is

THE DEVIL'S POOL.

A spot frequented first by the superstitious in the early days of the province, and now, for more than half a century, by artists and all lovers of nature. It is certainly a wild place; rocks are thrown together in great masses, and the long trunks of hemlocks and pines jut up from the darkness around the pool into the sunshine above.

The waters of a small tributary of the Wissahickon run into this pool, whose depth has been very suggestive to the superstitious minds which gave it its name.

The place is very readily accessible, and artists' sketches through our galleries have made it widely known. It was the scene of an engagement during the battle of Germantown, and its waters once had stains best now forgotten.

THE road reaches, a quarter of a mile beyond this bridge,

VALLEY GREEN.

Here the hills open out into the sunlight, and a stone bridge with strong buttresses winds across the stream. The bridge has one arch, and the arch and shadow on bright days (so clear is the reflection) seem one piece of masonry, an entire oval.

The transition from the close surroundings of the road below this point, to the widening hills beyond it, is very pleasing. The hotel here is a favorite stopping-place for carriages passing through this portion of the Park.

HALF a mile further, on the left-hand side of the road, under rocks, covered with ferns and wild-flowers, is a marble water-basin.

THE FIRST FOUNTAIN.

This is the first drinking-fountain erected in Philadelphia. It bears date 1854. A clear, cold mountain spring constantly fills the basin. On a slab above it are cut the words "Pro bono publico," and below, "Esto perpetua" (For the public good; Let it remain forever); which liberal desire and prayer the dedication of these grounds, after sixteen years, has invisibly, though not less really, lettered over every spring along the borders of the stream. "Cast thy bread upon the waters, for thou shalt find it after many days."

This fountain was the joint offering, to public use, of John Cook, by whom it was erected, and Charles Magarge, the owner of the spring. They donated this summer (1871) the fountain, and ground around it sufficient for its convenient use, to the Park Commissioners.

HALF a mile further, on the opposite side of the stream, looms grandly up,

INDIAN ROCK.

Here the stream enters a deep gorge. The hills tower almost perpendicularly, and the place has the solemn stillness of the shores of some far-off waters in the yet unbroken wilderness. A few huge rocks lie in the bed of the creek, but make no eddies in the water. The woods, clothing the inclosing steeps, bury their shadows in its dark surface. The rock, plainly seen from the road, very wild, grand, and lofty, crowns the summits of the eastern range of hills. It is shaped like a fireplace or a pulpit, square, with a deep cavity or hollow in its front. On its top stands the rude figure of an Indian, set there in remembrance of the last chief of the aborigines (the Lenni Lenape tribe) on these grounds. This chief, with forty other Indians, mostly women (the men had gone before), left this section about the time of the Revolution. They had remained long after the others of their tribe on these old hunting-grounds, but they had kept their savage nature and costume unchanged. The chief, with his blanket wrapped about him, and his tall plume of feathers on his brow, strode before; and the women, with their packs strapped across their backs and across their foreheads, followed after. So they joined the others in their journey toward the setting sun,

> "To the land of the Dacotahs,
> To the land of the hereafter."

Is it hard in this wild place still to imagine their light canoes stealing along through the evening or morning shadows?

Tedyuscung, whose name this rude figure improperly bears, was no true savage— was litigious, was frequently drunk, and showed also other evidences of a tendency to lapse into civilization.

THE road continues on a mile further, through the same general character of scenery, to the northern limits of the Park, at Thorp's mill lane, which crosses a bridge and by a steep ascent reaches

CHESTNUT HILL.

This hill is the site of many of the best suburban residences of Philadelphia. Here all the wild scenery of the Wissahickon, so closely shut in, opens outward over broad tracts of farm-land and distant mountains. It is a fitting terminus to this section, affording a view northward as grand in its character as from Mount Prospect over the lower section of the Park; each completing the idea, conceived in the appropriation of these grounds, to lead the visitor from attraction to attraction, and close with an effect in nature which leaves nothing to desire.

THE HOMES AND PERSONAGES

OF

FORMER TIMES.

SAMUEL BRECK.

A golden link of the days of the Revolution and our own times.

Mr. Breck was born in Boston, in 1771. He was educated near Toulouse, in Languedoc, in the Royal and Military School of Sorenze. His instructors were Benedictine monks. He remained at this school from his eleventh until his sixteenth year. His companions were the Prince de Carignan, ancestor of the King of Sardinia, several Italian and Spanish noblemen, Dessaix, and others, whose lives passed away into obscurity or ended in the violence of revolutions.

His own life was kept for gentler and better uses.

After a sojourn in his native place, he again visited Europe in the dark dawn of the French Revolution. He saw the King, Queen, and the Dauphin, the prisoners of the populace, about to expiate their predecessors' crimes. He saw the old teachers and pupils he loved driven from their ancient seat of learning, some to perish in the September massacres, some themselves to urge on the tide of crime.

These scenes made the quiet and calm progress of our Republic intensely dear to him.

He lived at Sweet Brier thirty-eight years. In the leisure hours of his business he cultivated here the sciences, the arts of music and design, and was foremost in every good work.[1]

"Farmer Breck," as his good friend and neighbor, Judge Peters, always called him, had here a model place; and while the Judge theorized, and saw the State rise through his theories to wealth, Farmer Breck, in their practical application, made his place a marvellous example of their value.

He gave a due proportion of his life to public affairs.

He served four years in the State Senate, where he laid the foundation of our system of internal improvements, and further made his name memorable by his bill for the final emancipation of the slaves in Pennsylvania.

---

[1] He was accomplished in all the graces of his time, and thoroughly read in its literature. In his life he never passed an idle hour, nor uttered an uncourteous word.

He served afterwards in the National Legislature (the 18th Congress), among the most memorable men our nation ever possessed, and in halcyon days of the Republic.

He again served in the State Senate, and there drew the bill for the establishment of the Common School System of Pennsylvania.

His services, from that time, were in positions of the very highest trust and importance in Philadelphia, and continuous to the year of his death.

Although a business man, Mr. Breck knew what the legitimate claims of business were, by what means money should be made, how much time should be given to its acquisition, and to what uses it should be applied. At the outset of his life, rather than live where illegitimate gain was sanctioned by common consent, he deliberately sacrificed an easy, safe, and rapid road to wealth which lay before him, and began with a small capital to make slower gains through longer years. He was a gentleman of the old school, and he preserved its courtesies on the street, in the counting-room, at the social board, with child and man, servant and dignitary of the State, the same. His salutations were formal, yet under them a gentle kindliness shone which lifted up the hearts of all to him in affection and reverence.

He was true to his party predilections, but with this preference ran evenly an earnest love for the whole country.

He was careful in all formal religious observances, but within he kept burning brightly that inner light, without which all religious observances are vain.

His life covered[1] the most momentous periods of our country's history. He welcomed Lincoln, the great representative of freedom of our generation, to this city in 1861, where he had also stood in the august pres-

---

[1] Born July 17, 1771. Died August 22, 1862, aged 91 years and 46 days.

ence of Washington. He had been held up a child in his nurse's arms to witness the smoke and flame of Bunker Hill, and he was yet living when Sumter's smouldering ruin lit the flames of civil war. Through all these long years he was changeless in his love and devotion to our institutions. His last words were (uttered among those dark days of civil war)—what of—my country.

There is something peculiarly appropriate in the selection of Sweet Brier as the children's play-ground, not only because he first gave legal direction to our common school system, but was a dear friend to little children. He was a constant visitor to the parish school of his church (the Episcopal), took the most lively interest in its progress, and by the sprightliness and benignity of his manner completely won the hearts of all the pupils. They looked forward to the day of his coming as to a holiday.

He was also one of the founders, for many years president, and to the last year of his life a visitor of the Institution for the Blind, and by these most afflicted of God's children best beloved. His step was recognized by them among all the others as he entered their hall.

LANSDOWNE MANSION.

The noble estate of Lansdowne contained two hundred acres, extending from Sweet Brier to Belmont and George's Hill.[1] The mansion was built before the Revolution. It was a grand structure for those times. A broad carriage drive led to it from an entrance beyond the Belmont Road, where formerly stood a large gateway. It had extensive conservatories, and the grounds were adorned with vases, fountains, and box cut in the formal style of the period. A private passage led from the mansion to the river. It was in later times the residence of Joseph

---

[1] During the occupancy of Philadelphia in the winter of 1777, the British had an encampment on these grounds.

Bonaparte, ex-King of Spain. Its last owner, prior to its purchase by the city, was the late Lord Ashburton. The mansion had been much neglected, although still in good preservation until a recent period. It was accidentally destroyed by boys with fireworks, celebrating the fourth of July, 1854.

JOHN PENN.

"The Honorable John Penn," [1] called "the Governor," was Lieutenant-Governor and Commander-in-Chief of the Province of Pennsylvania and Counties of New Castle, Kent, and Sussex on Delaware from 1763 to 1771 and from 1774 to 1776. He was a not unworthy representative of "the Founder;" his first act, followed by many like actions, was to carry out

---

[1] Cousin of John Penn, of Solitude.

that great man's intentions to the Indians who remained in the Province, and to protect them from outrage and violence. But his good record does not end there; during the whole term of his office, a prolonged one, he gave a wise and serious attention to the public affairs, and supported the honor and dignity of his family and of the Province. He maintained royal state on these grounds, and sumptuous surroundings, but also a clear record of wise government. His times were troublous ones; he was the last representative of the Founder who had authority here, and the last representative of kingly power in Pennsylvania. He bore up bravely against the coming violence of the storm of the Revolution, but, like some stately and unyielding tree, broke down before it. The bold free airs which swept about our land those days made sad havoc among the royal oaks transplanted to this uncongenial soil.[1]

[1] He retained throughout that season of trial the good-will of the worthy of all parties. After the dissolution of the government, though politically restrained, he was treated with the respect due to his exalted station and private worth. His successor was the sterling fisherman and patriot, Thomas Wharton. He was called from the old court-house, at the Baron Warner's, to preside over Pennsylvania, *vice* the fallen governor, in 1776.

John Penn resided in this mansion after the war; was visited by Washington in 1787. He died in Bucks County in this State, February 9, 1795, at the age of sixty-seven. His remains were taken back to England.

"The Penn estate," says the late Judge Conrad, "was the largest one ever sequestered in civil war; it was estimated at £10,000,000 sterling. The heirs received as a compensation from the British Government an annuity of £4000; and the State of Pennsylvania, in remembrance of the founder, awarded them £130,000." Their private estates were not divested, but have been held and inherited by succeeding members of the family down to our own day. "Solitude," as stated before, was purchased from them by the city. The governor, by his will, dated January 2, 1795, devised Lansdowne to his wife, Mrs. Anne Penn, and by subsequent conveyances through her title it also became the property of the city.

BELMONT IN THE OLDEN TIME.

JUDGE PETERS.

Richard Peters, the beloved friend of Washington, was born in this mansion, and died here August 22, 1828, at the age of eighty-four. He was the son of William Peters, and the nephew of Richard Peters, Secretary of the Land Office under the Penns. The father and son, in the Revolution severed in their opinions. The father adhered to the crown, returned to and died in England. Judge Peters at the outset ignored social, family, and business relations, assumed and adhered to the cause of the colonies. He was born in the den of the British lion, and in a good-humored manner bearded him there.

Judge Peters filled the office of Secretary of the Board of War during the Revolution; was a Representative in Congress, and had, at the time of his death, sat as a Judge of the United States District Court thirty-nine years. He was not alone distinguished as a patriot, a legislator, and a jurist, but in the department of agriculture he was the pioneer in those improvements which restored the wasting farm lands of this State. He sang the best song,[1] grave or gay, was the most noted wit of his times, and was also the most genial and hospitable of men.

[1] This fragment of a song in his clear handwriting lies before me; it was written at a meeting of the St. George's Society, September 28, 1774:—

>When Britain first, by Heaven's command,
>   Arose from out the azure main,
>This was the charter of the land,
>   And guardian angels sang this strain;
>   Rule, Britannia, rule the waves,
>   Britons never will be slaves.
>
>Let us, your sons, by freedom warmed,
>   Your own example keep in view;
>'Gainst tyranny be ever armed,
>   Tho' we our tyrants find—in you.
>   Rule, Britannia, rule the waves,
>   But never make your children slaves.
>
>With justice and with wisdom reign,
>   We then with thee will firmly join
>To make thee mistress of the main,
>   And all the shore it circles thine.
>   Rule, Britannia, rule the waves,
>   We're subjects still, but not your slaves.

A portion of the Judge's song of the Treaty Tree may be also appropriately quoted here:—

>Whilst the natives our forests in freedom shall roam,
>Thy remembrance they'll cherish through ages to come.
>Tho' sorrows their bosoms should oft overwhelm,
>With delight they'll reflect on *good Onas's Elm*.
>
>For that patron of justice and peace there displayed
>His most welcome good tidings, beneath its fair shade,

And furnished examples to all future times,
That Justice and Peace may inhabit all climes.

The *Oak* may be fam'd for its uses in war,
Or wafting wealth's idols to regions afar;
But the Elm bears no part in such objects as these,
Its employment is solely in fabrics of peace.

The *Olive* abounds where stern despots bear rule,
And their slaves pluck its products in Poverty's school;
But the *Elm* delights most in the mountains and dells,
Where *Man* is ne'er shackled, and Liberty dwells.

Tho' time has devoted our tree to decay,
The sage lessons it witness'd survive to our day,
May our trustworthy statesmen, when called to the helm,
Ne'er forget the wise *Treaty* held under our *Elm*.

Many anecdotes of Judge Peters are preserved in the manuscript of his biographer. They were a constant glimmer on the full deep flow of his earnest, enduring life. On the occasion of a brewer's death, when a dull man expressed surprise to the Judge because the brewer seemed to have been in good health: True, he was, said the Judge, a *stout* man. What could then have carried him off? said the dull questioner. Something *ated* him, and the *beer* carried him off, said the Judge. Ah! said the questioner: I did not know he drank. Nor did I, either, said the Judge, slowly shaking his head and walking away.

When the Judge's health began to fail, a report of his death got into circulation and produced general sorrow. He was riding, and was met by a stranger, who told him the sad news. Well, said the Judge to the astonished man, I, for one, am very glad to *hear* it. I have lived very long, but I never thought I'd live long enough to hear that that man was dead.

In his 76th year, dining with the Cincinnati Society, he saw that, of the 300 original members, but 40 remained. I am the oldest survivor, he said, cheerfully, and as this is a military association which places the senior officer in the rear of the procession, I shall take my place there, and so see you all out, and reach the dismal goal last. Seeing Smith, who had become entirely bald, he said: Smith, you must be a very happy man. Why, said Smith, innocently. Because, said he, Smith, there's not a hair between your head and heaven.

Among the guests of Judge Peters assembled in this mansion were the Chevalier de la Luzerne, the French Minister, whose house was at the Falls, Franklin, "Christian Samuel," Rittenhouse the astronomer, Bartram, President Wharton, and distinguished men of science from Europe. Lafayette, while in Philadelphia, on his return to this country as the nation's guest in 1824, was constantly with the Judge, and passed much of his time at this house. The Baron de Steuben, Inspector-General during the Revolution, was on relations of much intimacy with the Judge, and, whenever he was in Philadelphia, visited his house. Here also Talleyrand and Louis Philippe were received. Robert Morris, the Count de Survilliers, John Penn the governor, Alexander J. Dallas the advocate, whose house was near the Falls, John Adams, and, before all these, the author of the great Declaration,[1] were his neighbors.

---

[1] During Washington's administration, Thomas Jefferson lived below the Park limits at Gray's Ferry. He continued to reside there until he retired from public life in December, 1793, and these fair shores witnessed an interview in those days of our transition from monarchical ideas following the close of the Revolution, which shows the influence Washington held even over this great man. Jefferson, then Secretary of State, had finally determined to resign his office; nor was it credited, so decided were the positions he had taken, that his determination was alterable. Washington, unbending from the place of his superior rank, visited him, and in a long interview (August 6th, 1793) beside these waters besought him to remain in the discharge of his office. Jefferson had then written to his life-long friend and companion Madison (June 9th, 1793), in a spirit of utter weariness of public affairs. "The motion of my blood," he said in this letter, "no longer keeps time with the turmoil of the world, my happiness lies in the lap and love of my family, in my books and in the society of my neighbors, in an interest and affection in every bud that opens and breath that blows around me. I am worn down with fruitless labor." To Washington he yielded. It is a pleasant recollection that this great instructor of his age, who so loved also the passing air and opening flower, had for that then worn-down spirit the relief of these fair scenes of nature, and that the scenes themselves are thus associated with his name and widening influence over our race.

Washington's memory is the most sacred legacy of these fair grounds; the biographer of Judge Peters (the late Samuel Breck) writes: "Whenever a morning of leisure permitted that great man to drive to Belmont, it was his constant habit to do so; in its beautiful gardens, beneath the shadows of the lofty hemlocks, he would sequester himself from the world, the cares and torments of business, and enjoy a recreative and unceremonious intercourse with the Judge."

On occasions of ceremony, however, at receptions and entertainments, Washington maintained surroundings of state in keeping with his time and military habitudes, although incongruous with these later days. The old shell of the royal era remained long after the soul and heart of the thing were gone. In the details of his household, also, he was very stately, and among all the equipages which rolled up to the door of Judge Peters's mansion, his was the most decisive in its appointments. His coach, which is still in good preservation, was of a cream color, drawn by six horses of the old dominion stock. His motto was engraved on the harness plates; his crest on the panels; his postilions wore bright tasselled caps, and his coachman maintained a dignity and style in perfect keeping with the whole.

He rode here also on the white charger which bore him in the Revolution, sometimes with attendants, sometimes alone.

THE SOLITUDE.

The Solitude Estate now forms a portion of the Zoölogical Society's grounds.

The Villa, as its first owner described it, "near Philadelphia, built by me while I resided in America," was erected in 1785 by John Penn—the poet, a grandson of the Founder. It remained in the Penn family until its purchase by the Park Commissioners. The house, except from age, remains quite as the builder left it, and is a pleasant poet's home. It has a small drawing-room; a room adjoining, which served both for a hall and sitting-room; a chamber with an alcove, for his hours of rest; a library, where at once he was his author and auditor; and deep and roomy cellars for his wine. This fortunate poet's old bookcases, set in the wall, give the same quiet to the room they did the days when he lived there. His sunny sitting-room is quite the same. The secret door by which he shut himself from visits of intrusive friends, closes as quietly to as it did so many years ago. The life of the builder of this mansion is in strong contrast with the severe and broad virtues of William Penn and the other great historic characters who have made these grounds memorable. John Penn, the poet, loved solitude, but he made this place an enviable solitude; and though he loved his own poems and read them all day long, and though they had no other reader, yet they show what guests assembled in his solitude. Dante was there; Chaucer, "the well of English undefiled;" Petrarch and Tasso; and Anacreon. Here he sat dreaming through the summer days, the leisure days of a life which all was leisure. In one of the volumes of his poems, printed in London in 1801, he gives a view of this villa, of which the above is a fac-simile, and calls it "The Solitude." The white dove he has had the artist picture flying close along the lawn had been a favorite bird, and he there deplores, with Anacreon's pleasant thoughts and in these old-time words and verse, its death.—

> "Thine, oft I said (nor hoped[1] so near thy end),
> Are all things round,[2] the grove, and cloudless sky;
> While cheers the enlivening ray, sport and enjoy;
> Thine are yon oaks that o'er the stream impend,
> And rocks that, as I stray with musing eye,
> Or wonder[3] from the shed,[4] can never cloy."

---

[1] Hope, expect.   [2] Round, around.   [3] Wonder, admire.   [4] Shed, door.

It is said he planted every tree about this house with his own hands; this there is reason to believe, and for the many trees which yet remain, and for that picture of the dove flying across the lawn, we keep his memory.

GRANVILLE JOHN PENN.

Granville John Penn, the great-grandson of the Founder, the last private owner of Solitude, and the last of the Founder's name, visited this country in 1851. His father in his time one of the most learned laymen of England, and himself a kindly old English gentleman, he was the recipient, from our old-time citizens and from the authorities, of suitable attentions. In acknowledgment of these attentions, he gave a collation at "The Solitude." It is interesting to remember that this house was the last property here of a family which was once the owner of the broad State of Pennsylvania; the descendants of a wise and good man, whose title, unlike so many others in this and other countries, was founded "in deeds of peace," kept with "unbroken faith." Mr. Penn wished that the city should become its owner, and keep it for the Founder's name. He did not live to see this pious wish fulfilled, which since his death, to our advantage, has been done. The sale of this property to the city, and the release by himself in 1852 of the render of a red rose at Christmas from the good people of Easton, closes the long account of that great Founder's name with ourselves; its own account on earth now also closed forever.

Granville John Penn died at Stoke Pogis, England, March 29, 1867. He was the last (save one since deceased) of that line.

GEORGE'S HILL.

Among the first and the most grateful of all the acquisitions by the Commissioners was this fine tract of ground. Soon after they began their labors they received a letter from Jesse George, an aged and estimable member of the Society of Friends, who, with his sister, were then its joint owners.

In the letter Jesse George stated that this property had been the uninterrupted home of his ancestors for many generations, and had retained very much the appearance it bore from the first settlement of the country. That, with a view of preserving it to their memory in the same rural condition in which they occupied it, he had declined all offers to sell it; but that considering the benefits of a public Park, and that a disposition of the property by him for that purpose would carry out his wishes for its preservation, he offered it to his fellow-citizens as a contribution to their pleasure-ground. Rebecca George joined with him in the same offer.

The Commissioners accepted this generous gift, reserving for these estimable persons, at their request, the undisturbed enjoyment during their lives of the water of a little brook which runs along the foot of the hill.

The tract comprises eighty-three acres. An oval concourse two hundred feet in diameter crowns its summit, which is two hundred and ten feet above the river.

The presentation of the ground was made 12mo. 11th, 1868. Jesse George survived his sister, and died at the old homestead adjoining the hill Feb. 14, 1873, aged 88 years.

Among the purposes entertained by the Commissioners, that to preserve and restore the mansions on these grounds is most approvable. All that helps to realize to us the days and actors of the Revolution is of much importance to our future. The narrow glass windows of this mansion are more precious to patriotic eyes than the broad plates of our era. The small rooms, with their low ceilings, and their open fireplaces, contending with wintry draughts, are more grateful to patriotic hearts than any lofty chambers of our present residences—for their occupants were the foremost men of our race, and their great work was for all time.

We have made marvellous advances in all appliances for material grandeur and convenience. We have substituted for their stately equipages moving palaces on the water and on the land as much grander and more costly, as those were than the lumbering wains of the laborers of their times. We have overlaid by railroads, and broken down by battles, the narrow lines of the thirteen old sovereignties, extended their area across the continent, and unified them to a nation. We have advanced higher the standard of freedom, until no slave toils on our soil. But we have given no better type of the uses of wealth, than the Financier of the Colonies. We have reached no farther in our theories of government than the Author of the Declaration. And among all our millions, and all the world's millions, there has never been reproduced a man in the likeness of the Leader of the Armies of the Revolution.

FLAGS OF THE SCHUYLKILL NAVY.

COMMODORE

VICE COMMODORE

1ST CLASS CHAMPION

2ND CLASS CHAMPION

3RD CLASS CHAMPION

UNIVERSITY

UNDINE

QUAKER CITY

PENNSYLVANIA

PHILADELPHIA

MALTA

CRESCENT

CLUBS UNATTACHED TO THE NAVY.

BACHELORS

PACIFIC

VESPER

THE SCHUYLKILL NAVY.

The boats are classified as follows:—

    FIRST CLASS . . . . Shells.
    SECOND CLASS . . . Outrigger Lapstreaks.
    THIRD CLASS . . . . Smooth Gunwale Barges.

The regulation size of flags is as follows:—

    For boat-house, 30 × 40 inches, bunting.
    " boats, 12 × 18 " silk, to be carried at the bow.
    " racing, 6 × 8 " " " "

THE PACIFIC BARGE CLUB.

Organized June 15, 1859. It is unattached to the Navy. Uniform: winter—pants dark blue cloth (Navy style), shirt black and scarlet striped, caps leather (skull); summer—pants white linen, hats straw. Number of members, active twenty, honorary four.

BOATS.

IMP . . . length, 42 feet; oars, 6; class, 3d; color, varnished Spanish cedar.
FLIRT . . " 38 " " 4; " 3d; " white cedar, painted.
WREN . . " 27 " double sculls; class, 1st; color, varnished Spanish cedar.

The Imp is considered the best boat of its class on the river; carries eighteen persons.

The club has an elegant model of the Wren, made by one of their members. It is twenty-seven inches long, of six different woods; complete in every particular, and fastened with five hundred and four copper rivets.

THE QUAKER CITY BARGE CLUB.

Organized October 20, 1858. Uniform: shirt blue, with white trimming and trefoil corners; cap blue, with name on front; jacket blue, with navy buttons; pants blue. Number of members, active thirty, honorary six. This club has held the first class champion flag for three successive years. It has also the second class champion flag for four-oared boats.

BOATS.

NAUTILUS	length, 48 feet;	oars, 4;	class, 1st;	color, varnished.
CYGNET	" 42 "	" 4;	" 2d;	" white.
BERTHA	" 25 "	double sculls;	class, 2d;	color, white.
SWAN	" 30 "	single "	" 1st;	paper.
SPIDER	" 17 "	" "	" "	"
IRIS	" 40 "	oars, 6;	" 3d;	color, white body.
WASP	" 40 "	" 4;	class, 1st;	paper.

These two clubs occupy the first of the range of barge-houses going from Fairmount. It is of stone, and was built in 1860. It is fifty-five feet long and thirty-five feet wide, divided into two compartments. The house has balconies at each end.

THE PENNSYLVANIA BARGE CLUB.

Was organized June 4, 1861, as the Atlantic Barge Club, and subsequently changed to this name. Uniform: dark blue shirt, dark blue pants, and leather cap. Active members twenty-five, contributors thirty. Among their boats is a twelve-inch paper shell, thirty-two feet long; weight, thirty-two pounds; built for and named Henry Coulter.

BOATS.

FALCON	length, 42 feet;	oars, 6;	class, 3d;	color, red, gold stripe.
STRANGER	" 38 "	" 4;	" 3d;	" black, gold stripe.
MERMAID	" 42 "	" 4;	" 2d;	" varnished.
CELIA	" 20 "	double sculls;	class, 2d;	color, red, black stripe.
JOHN CULIN	" 34½ "	single "	" 1st;	" varnished.
HENRY COULTER	" 32 "	" "	" 1st;	" " paper.
JOSIE	" 33½ "	" "	" 1st;	" " "

THE CRESCENT BOAT CLUB.

Organized December 1st, 1867. Uniform: for winter—dark navy blue coat, shirt, and trowsers, sailor cap with the club name; summer—straw hat, blue shirt and trowsers. Active members thirty-two, contributing eighteen.

BOATS.

INTREPID	length, 48 feet;	oars, 6;	class, 2d;	color, green, black stripe.				
IONE	" 42 "	" 6;	" 3d;	" crimson, gold stripe.				
SYLPH	" 25 "	double sculls;	class, 2d;	color, crimson, gold stripe.				
TURTLE	" 14½"	"	"	" 2d;	"	"	"	"
NEREID	" 22½"	"	"	" 2d;	"	"	"	"
OWLET	" 35 "	"	"	" 1st;	varnished.			
CRESCENT	" 42 "	oars, 4;	class, 1st;	color, "				
PETREL	" 25 "	single	" 1st;	"	"			
FROLIC	" 28 "	"	" 1st;	"	"			
AH SIN	" 28 "	"	" 1st;	"	"			
CLAM	" 15 "	"	scull; class, 2d; black.					

The Pennsylvania and Crescent Clubs own and occupy the same building (the second of the houses); it is of stone, fifty by forty feet, two stories in height, with a Mansard roof.

Each club has entirely separate apartments, the boat-rooms on the first floor being separated by a stone partition-wall. In consequence of the higher grade on the Park front, the house is entered on the second floor, a six feet wide hall running between the dressing and reception rooms, on each side. The Crescent occupy the southwest side of the building. Their rooms are plastered alike, roughcast tinted, with gilt cornices. The dressing-room is furnished with closets for each member, a six-light chandelier, side lights, mirror, &c.; the wood-work finished in oak, and the floor oiled and varnished.

The reception-room is finished in walnut, has a four-light chandelier, the furniture walnut and green rep; the windows are curtained, the floor carpeted, and the walls decorated with paintings. A glass door opens out upon a balcony which extends along the entire river front of the house.

The above-mentioned clubs were the first to introduce this style of building, affording the most commodious boat-houses in this country.

BACHELORS' BARGE CLUB.

Organized on the 4th of July, 1853; it is unattached to the Navy. Uniform: blue flannel shirt, bound with single white braid, gilt buttons on front and on the cuffs; blue cloth pants, heavy blue cloth pea-jacket, blue cloth navy cap lettered Bachelor, and black silk neckerchief. Summer: straw hat, black ribbon streamer and gilt letters Bachelor in front. Twenty-nine active members, twenty-three honorary members.

BOATS.

BACHELOR	length, 52 feet;	oars, 6;	class, 1st;	color, varnished.	
LINDA	" 50 "	" 6;	" 3d;	"	"
LOTUS	" 42 "	" 4;	" 2d;	" green, gold stripe.	
GAZELLE	" 25 "	double sculls;	class, 2d;	color, varnished.	
BRAT	" 30 "	one pair sculls	" 1st;	"	"
CUB	" 32 "	" " "	" 1st;	"	"
——	" — "	oars, 4;	class, 1st;	color, varnished.	

The house of this club is the third of the boat-houses; a neat brown stone, Gothic edifice, two stories high, with balconies. It is fifty-five feet long, and twenty-five feet wide. It, as also the others, have the same general style and arrangements with the first of the houses.

UNIVERSITY BARGE CLUB.

Organized April 25, 1854, by classmen of the University of Pennsylvania. Uniform: red flannel shirt bound with black braid, jet buttons, and falling collar with black silk stars in the corners; black pantaloons in winter, white in summer; black patent-leather belt with U. B. C. in raised plated letters; black silk necktie; black morocco jockey cap in winter, and in summer a white Mackinaw straw hat bound with black, with University in gold letters on the ribbon, and the initials of the owner painted in black on the crown. Forty-two active members, thirty-six honorary. It is now the senior club of the Navy.

BOATS.

UNIVERSITY, length, 48 feet; oars, 4; class, 1st; color, varnished.
HESPERUS   "   36 "   " 4; " 1st;   "   "
LUCIFER .   "   45 "   " 6; " 2d;   " white, black and red stripe.

PHILADELPHIA BARGE CLUB.

Organized December 8, 1862; incorporated July 13, 1870. Uniform: a plain double-breasted shirt of blue flannel, covered buttons, and white flannel trowsers, pea-jacket, and skullcap of same material as shirt. Number of members, seventeen active, and nine honorary.

BOATS.

FAUGH A BALLAGH, length, 42 feet; oars, 6; class, 2d; color, varnished.
NO NAME . . . . .   "   22 "   double sculls; class, 2d; color, varnished.
MIST . . . . "   41 "   oars, 4; class, 1st; paper; weight 100 pounds.
LORELEI. . . . . . "   37 "   "   "   3d; —— color, varnished.
FLY . . . .   "   17 "   single scull; class, 2d; —— color, varnished.

The University and Philadelphia occupy jointly the fourth of the houses. It is 42 × 57 feet; built of West Chester green stone, Mansard roof; bay windows on the Park side, and is fitted up with dressing and reception rooms, balcony extending over the whole river front, and over the bay windows on the Park side.

MALTA BOAT CLUB.

Organized February, 1860. The uniform is blue shirt trimmed with red cord, blue pants, blue sack-coat with navy buttons, and blue cap. Members, thirty-two active, three contributing, one honorary. In addition to the boats as classified, this club is building two others.

BOATS.

HIAWATHA . . . length, 43 feet; oars, 6; class, 2d; color, green, gold stripe.
MINNEHAHA . .   "   35 "   " 6; "   3d; "   orange, gold stripe.
COLUMBIA . . .   "   45 "   " 6; "   2d; "   varnished.
IDALIA . . . . .   "   46 "   " 4; "   1st; "   "
WASP . . . . . .   "   18 "   double sculls; class, 3d; color, varnished.

VESPER BOAT CLUB.

Organized February 22, 1865. It is unattached to the Navy. The uniform is dark blue flannel shirt (U. S. seaman's pattern), dark blue pants, cap, and pea-jacket. Members, thirty-six active, ten honorary.

BOATS.

VESPER . . . . length, 42½ feet; oars, 6; class, 3d; color, white, gold stripe.
VENTURE . . .   "   37 "   " 4; "   3d; "   varnished.
ONWARD . . .   "   37½ "   " 4; "   2d; "   red, gold stripe.
VAGABOND . .   "   26 "   double sculls; class, 2d; color, varnished.
VOLANT . . .   "   42 "   oars, 4; class, 1st; color, varnished.
Two single working boats.

The house of the Vesper and Malta is the fifth in order. Is an ornate structure of stone.

THE UNDINE BARGE CLUB.

Organized May 9, 1856. Uniform: blue flannel shirt with white trimmings, blue pants, straw hat, black ribbon with word Undine in gilt letters. Members, fifty-eight active, ten honorary. A record of one of its members, from August, 1862, to January, 1871, shows an actual distance pulled of over 11,481 miles. The Club's record shows that its boats are out from five hundred to seven hundred times yearly. For the year 1868, five hundred and fifty-one times; 1869, seven hundred and forty-five times; 1870, six hundred and fifty times. The greatest number of miles rowed by a member was in 1866, 1402 miles; in 1867, 1224; in 1868, 1281; in 1869, 2643; in 1870, 1202. In 1868, twenty-four members rowed an average of 443 miles; in 1869, eighteen members an average of 551; in 1870, twenty-two members an average of 410.

This Club occupies a portion of the Skating Club's house.

BOATS.

SCUD	length, 43 feet;	oars, 4;	class, 1st;	color, varnished.			
WHISPER	" 42 "	" 4;	" 1st;	" "			
NEW ATALANTA .	" 45 "	" 6;	" 2d;	" "			
OLD ATALANTA .	" 40 "	" 6;	" 2d;	" blue, gold stripe.			
UNDINE	" 40 "	" 6;	" 3d;	" " " "			
FAWN	" 23½ "	double sculls;	class, 2d;	color, blue, gold stripe.			
CRAB	" 17 "	1 pair "	" 2d;	" " " "			
SELAH	" 31 "	" "	" 1st;	" varnished.			
RIPPLE	" "	single "	" 1st;	" "			
"C. V"	" 20	" "	" "	" "			
TERRAPIN	" 17	" " .	" 2d;	" "			
———	" 34 "	double sculls;	" 1st;	" "			

ROWING TIME.

The best time as yet made on the Schuylkill is—

June 1, 1867.	HESPERUS	4 oars,	1st class	20 min.	03 sec.,	3 miles.
" 1, "	BACHELOR	6 "	1st "	20 "	38 "	"
" 1, "	IRIS	6 "	3d "	19 "	32 "	"
" 15, "	NEW ATALANTA	6 "	2d "	18 "	54 "	"
July 1869.	HIAWATHA	6 "	2d "	18 "	02 "	"
" "	MINNEHAHA	6 "	3d "	19 "	05 "	"
Oct. 1, 1870.	QUAKER CITY	4 "	1st "	19 "	26 "	"
" 5, "	SINGLE SCULL.			20 "		"

The distance from Turtle Rock to Girard Avenue Bridge is 2060 feet; to the rock just beyond the Connecting Railway Bridge on the west bank, ¾ a mile; to a point half-way between the lower end of the island and the steamboat landing on the west bank, 1 mile; to the Columbia Bridge, 1 mile and 1400 feet; to the middle of Peters Island, 1⅞ mile; to Berkenbine's clearing, 2 miles; to Laurel Hill landing, 2 miles and 2300 feet; to a long white house on the west bank, half-way between the landing and the Falls Bridge, 2½ miles; to the Falls Bridge, 2 miles and 4600 feet. The stake boat was placed here at the race, October, 1870.

LIST OF TREES AND HERBACEOUS PLANTS IN THE PARK WHICH FLOWER IN MAY.

TREES AND SHRUBS.

ACER. *Maple.*
  saccharinum......Sugar.
  dasycarpum......Silver-leaved.
  platanoides......Norway Maple.
  campestre......English Maple.
  pseudo platanus......English Sycamore.
  rubrum......Red Maple.
NEGUNDO. *Box Elder.*
  fraxinifolium......Ash-leaved.
CELTIS. *Beaver wood.*
  occidentalis......Western.
FRAXINUS. *Ash.*
  Americana......American.
  juglandifolia......Walnut-leaved.
  sambucifolia......Elder-leaved.
ÆSCULUS. *Horse Chestnut.*
  hippocastanum......Common.
  Ohioensis......Ohio.
  rubicunda......Ruddy.
  pallida......Pale-flowered.
PAVIA. *Pavia.*
  flava......Yellow.
  humilis......Humble.
CERASUS. *Cherry.*
  multiplex pendula......Weeping d. fl.
  Virginiana......Virginia Bird Cherry.
CERCIS. *Judas Tree.*
  Canadensis......Canadian Tree.
BETULA. *Birch.*
  alba......White.
  nigra......Black.
CASTANEA. *Chestnut.*
  vesca......Common.
CORYLUS. *Hazel.*
  Americana......American.
HALESIA. *Silver Bell.*
  tetraptera......Four-winged.
LAURUS. *Laurus.*
  sassafras......Sassafras Tree.
  benzoin......Spice Bush.
LIRIODENDRON. *Tulip Tree.*
  tulipifera......Tulip Flowering.
MORUS. *Mulberry.*
  alba......White.
  rubra......Red.

NYSSA. *Sour Gum Tree.*
  vallosa......Hairy.
DIOSPYROS. *Persimmon.*
  Virginiana......Common Virginian.
SALIX. *Willow.*
  fragilis......Brittle.
  nigra......Black.
  vitellina......Golden.
  Russelliana......Russell's.
  laurifolia......Laurel-leaved.
  caprea pendula......Kilmar'k Weeping.
  rosem rinafolia......Rosemary-leaved.
CYDONIA. *Quince.*
  Japonica......Japan.
  Japonica alba......White.
  vulgaris......Common.
KALMIA. *Kalmia.*
  latifolia......Broad-leaved.
FORSYTHIA. *Golden Bell.*
  viridissima......Green-leaved.
ZANTHOXYLUM. *Toothache.*
  fraxineum......Ash-leaved.
STAPHYLA. *Bladder-nut.*
  trifolium......Three-leaved.
SYRINGA. *Lilac Tree.*
  vulgaris......Common.
  alba......White.
  persica......Persian.
CALYCANTHUS. *Sweet Shrub.*
  florida......Flowering.
ECONYMUS. *Burning Bush.*
  atropurpureus......Dark Purple.
  Americana......American.
LIGUSTRUM. *Privet.*
  communis......Common.
RIBES. *Ribes.*
  aureum......Golden-flowered Currant.
CORNUS. *Dogwood.*
  florida......White-flowered.
  sericea......Silky.
CRATÆGUS. *Hawthorn.*
  oxycantha......English.
  crusgalli......Cockspur.
FAGUS. *Beech.*
  sylvatica......Common wood.

QUERCUS. *Oak.*
  nigra......Black.
  falcata......Spanish
  alba......White.
  discolor......Two-colors.
  rubra......Red.
  prinus......Chestnut.
  quercitron......Dyer's.
  heterophylla......Various-leaved.
CARPINUS. *Hornbeam.*
  Americana......American.
PLATANUS. *Buttonwood.*
  occidentalis......Western.
JUGLANS. *Walnut.*
  regia......Royal.
  nigra......Black.
  compressa......Shelbark.
  macrocarpa......Large-fruited.
  alba......Common Hickory.
  porcina......Pignut "
TILIA. *Linden.*
  Americana......American.
  rubra......Red.
  Europea......European.
PAULOWNIA. *Paulownia.*
  imperialis......Imperial.
BROUSSONETIA. *P. Mulberry.*
  papyrifera......Paper.
GLEDITSCHIA. *Locust.*
  tricanthos......Three-spined.
  inermis......Thornless.
CHIONANTHUS. *W. Fringe.*
  Virginica......Virginian.
GYMNOCLADUS. *Ky. Coffee.*
  Canadense......Canadian.
ALNUS. *Alder.*
  glauca......Mealy-leaved.

MAGNOLIA. *Magnolia.*
  cordata......Heart-shaped leaf.
  tripetela......Umbrella Tree.
  purpurea......Purple-flowered.
  purpurea gracilis......Slen. purple-flow'd.
AMYGDALUS. *Almond.*
  persica flore pleno......D. Persian.
AZALEA. *Rosebay.*
  viscosa......Clammy.
BERBERIS. *Barberry.*
  vulgaris......Common.
  atropurpurea......Dark Purple.
SPIREA. *Spirea.*
  prunifolium......Plum-leaved.
  Reevesii......White-flowered.
KERRIA. *Kerria.*
  Japonica......Japan.
DEUTZIA. *Deutzia.*
  scabra......Rough.
  gracilis......Slender.
  crenata fl. pl......Double Pink-flowered.
VIBURNUM. *Viburnum.*
  prenifolium......Plum-leaved.
  lantanoides......Lantana-like.
  oxycocus......Tree Cranberry.
WEIGELIA. *Weigelia.*
  amabilis......Lovely.
  rosea......Rosy.
PHILADELPHUS. *Mock Orange.*
  coronarius......Common.
  grandiflorus......Grand-flowering.
RHUS. *Mist Tree.*
  cotinus......Wild Olive.
LONICERA. *Honeysuckle.*
  tartarica......Tartarian.
  alba......White.
  xylosteum......English Fly.
GLYCINA. }
WISTARIA. } *Glycinia.*

HERBACEOUS PLANTS.

ERIGERON. *Plantain.*
  bellidifolium......Daisy-flowered.
PANAX. *Ginseng.*
  quinquifolia......Five-leaved.
  pentstemon......Pentstemon.
  pubescens......Hairy.
OXALIS. *Wood Sorrel.*
  acetosella......Common.
  violacea......Violet-flowered.
  stricta......Upright.

CARDAMINE. *Lady Smock.*
  Pennsylvanica......Pennsylvanian.
DENTARIA. *Tooth Wort.*
  laciniata......Jagged.
ARABIS. *Wall Cress.*
  falcata. Sickle-pod.
TRADESCANTIA. *Spider Wort.*
  Virginica......Virginian.
  rosea......Rose-colored.

VERONICA. *Speedwell.*
  setigera......Bristly.
  arvensis......Cornfield.
  serpyllifolia......Serpyllium-leaved.
CONVALLARIA. *Lily of Valley.*
  majalis......May.
SMILACINA. *Smilacina.*
  racemosa......Racemose flowered.
  trifolia......Three-leaved.
  bifolia......Two-leaved.
POLYGONATUM. *Solomon's.*
  multiflorum......Many-flowered.
SAXIFRAGA. *Saxafraga.*
  Pennsylvanica......Pennsylvanian.
  Virginica......Virginian.
HOUSTONIA. *Houstonia.*
  cerulea......Blue-flowered.
CLAYTONIA. *Claytonia.*
  Virginica......Virginian.
HEPATICA. *Hepatica.*
  triloba......Three-lobed.
ALSINE. *Chickweed.*
  pubescens......Pubescent.
  media......Mediate.
ERYTHRONIUM. *Violet.*
  Americanum......American.
BARBAREA. *Mustard.*
  precox......Early.
CORYDALIS. *Corydalis.*
  lutea......Yellow.
FUMARIA. *Fumaria.*
  officinalis......Officinale.
SENECIO. *Groundsel.*
  aurea......Yellow.
VALERIANELLA. *Lambs-lettuce.*
  radiata......Radiated.
  olitoria......Salad.
AQUILEGIA. *Columbine.*
  Canadense......Canadian.
VIOLA. *Violet.*
  pedata......Pedate.
  blanda......White.
  lanceolata......Lance-leaved.
  hastata......Halberd-leaved.
  saggitata......Snow-leaved.
  rotundifolia......Round-leaved.
  trifoliata lutea......Three-leaved Yellow.
  striata......Striped.
  arvensis......Field.
CHELIDONIUM. *Celandine.*
  majus......Large.
ANEMONE. *Anemone.*
  thalictroides......Thalictrum-like.
  nemorosa......Grove.

SINAPIS. *Mustard.*
  nigra......Common Black.
LEONTODON. *Dandelion.*
  taraxacum......Common.
HIERACIUM. *Hawkweed.*
  venosum......Veined-leaf.
RUMEX. *Dock.*
  crispa......Curled.
  obtusifolium......Obtuse-leaved.
KRIGIA. *Krigia.*
  Virginica......Virginian.
MUSCARIA. *Grape Hyacinth.*
  botryoides......Botrys-like.
CHEROPHYLLUM. *Chervil.*
  Canadense......Canadian.
SMYRNIUM. *Alexanders.*
  trifoliatum......Three-leaved.
  purpurea......Purple.
TRILLIUM. *Trillium.*
  cerneum......Drooping-flowered.
ARALIA. *Aralia.*
  nudicaulis......Naked-stemmed.
THALICTRUM. *E. Meadow Rue.*
  diœcium......Diœcious.
CAULOPHYLLUM. *Caulophyllum.*
  thalictroides......Thalictrum-like.
  asarum......Ginger Root.
  Canadense......Canadian.
COCHLEARIA. *Scurvygrass.*
  armoracea......Horseradish.
LAMIUM. *Archangel.*
  ampelicaule......Stem-clasp Hen.
GALIUM. *Bedstraw.*
  Aparine......Cleavers.
  tinctorium......Dyers.
PODOPHYLLUM. *May Apple.*
  peltatum......Peltate leaf.
CHRYSOSPLENIUM. *Saxafrage.*
  oppositifolium......Opposite leaved.
RANUNCULUS. *Crowfoot.*
  Pennsylvanica......Pennsylvanian.
  bulbosa......Bulbous.
  fascicularis......Bundled.
  abortiva......Abortive.
SYMPLOCARPUS. *Skunk Cabbage.*
  fœtidus......Fetid.
  angustifolium......Narrow-spathed.
ARUM. *Arum.*
  triphyllum......Three-leaved.
  atrorubens......Dark Purple Stalked.
DRABA. *Draba.*
  verna......Vernal.
CHRYSANTHEMUM. *Chrysanthemum.*
  leucanthemum......Ox-eye Daisy.

GLECHOMA. *Ground Ivy.*
  rotundifolia......Round-leaved
  hederacea......Common.
POTENTILLA. *Cinquefoil.*
  sarmentosa......Twigged.
  Canadensis......Canadian.
FRAGARIA. *Strawberry.*
  vesca......Wood.
GERANIUM. *Crane's Bill.*
  maculatum......Spotted.
ORNITHOGALUM. *Star of Bethlehem.*
  umbellatum......Umbellated.
EPIGÆA. *Ground Laurel.*
  repens......Creeping.
SALIVA. *Sage.*
  lyrata......Lyre-shaped.
MALAXIS. *Malaxis.*
  lilifolium......Lily-leaved.

NASTURTIUM. *Nasturtium.*
  officinalis......Officinale.
MEDEOLA. *Indian Cucumber.*
  Virginica......Virginian.
SISYRYNCHIUM. *Blue-eyed Grass.*
  anceps......Iris-leaved.
HEUCHERA. *Arum Root.*
  Americana......American.
PLANTAGO. *Plantain.*
  major......Large.
  Virginica......Virginian.
  lanceolata......Lance-leaved.
  crassifolia......Thick-leaved.
TRIFOLIUM. *Clover.*
  pratense......Common Red.
  repens......White Clover.
  campestre......Slender Wood.
ANTENNARIA. *Ant.*
  plantaginea......Plantain-leaved.

LIST OF WORKS OF ART.

Statue of Justice, at Fairmount, carved by Rush.
     "   Wisdom,   "   "   "

The Graff Memorial,   "

Marble antique,   "

Leda and the Swan,   "   carved by Rush.

Emblematic composition on wheel-houses, carved by Rush.

Marble Fountain, from a Borghese palace, Rome.

The first fountain on the Wissahickon, marble.

The Indian (roughly cut in wood).

Two Pegasus Groups, at Belmont Offices.

Venus risen from the Bath, cast finished by Dr. Rush.

Statue of Lincoln, on the Plaza.

Night, at George's Hill.

The Wolves, at Lansdowne.

The Dying Lioness.

Il Penseroso, in the Picture Gallery.

Compiled to October, 1875.

COMPARATIVE SIZE OF PARKS IN EUROPE AND AMERICA.

FROM THE MOST RELIABLE SOURCES.

Park at the Hague, 200 acres. Alameda, City of Mexico, 12 acres. Park at Munich, 320 acres. Peel, Manchester, 32 acres. Petit Park, Versailles, 1280 acres. Palais Royal, 10 acres. Tuileries, 50 acres. Luxembourg, 160 acres. Champs Elysée, 225 acres. The Bois de Boulogne, 2158 acres. Grosse Garden, Saxony, 800 acres. Schwebgingen, near Heidelberg, 300 acres. Schloss Garden, Stuttgard, 560 acres. Hof Garden, Munich, 500 acres. Thier Garden, Berlin, 200 acres. Djurgard, Stockholm, 480 acres. The Prater, Vienna, 2500 acres. The Summer Garden, near St. Petersburg, 480 acres. Boboli, Florence, 200 acres. Tzarsco Selo, near St. Petersburg, 350 acres. Sweetzingen, near Mannheim, 100 acres. Richmond Hill, 2468 acres. Lambeth, 250 acres. Kew Garden, 684 acres. Arboretum, Derby, 50 acres. Meadows, Edinburgh, 200 acres. Phœnix Park, Dublin, 1752 acres. Birkenhead, Liverpool, 185 acres. Kensington Gardens, 35 acres. Buckingham Palace, 40 acres. Hyde Park, 389 acres. St. James's Park, 59 acres. Green Park, 55 acres. Regent's Park, 450 acres. Norfolk, Sheffield, 20 acres. Primrose Hill, 50 acres. Greenwich Park, 200 acres. Baxter, Dundee, 37 acres. Victoria, 300 acres. Crystal Palace, Edinburgh, 200 acres. Battersea, 175 acres. Albert Park, 409 acres. Kensington Park, 262 acres. Chiswick Gardens, 33 acres. Windsor Little Park, 500 acres. Windsor Great Park, 1800 acres. Hampton Court, 1872 acres. Green, Glasgow, 121 acres. Prince's Park, Liverpool, 90 acres. Washington, South Park, 150 acres. Hartford, Central, 46 acres. New York, Central Park, 862 acres. The other New York public grounds are—The Battery, 30 acres; City Hall Park, 10¼ acres; Washington Parade Ground, 9¾ acres; Union Square, 4 acres; Stuyvesant Park, 4 acres; Tompkins Square, 10¼ acres; Madison Square, 7 acres; St. John's Park, 4 acres; Gramercy Park, 1¾ acre. Brooklyn, Prospect, 550 acres. Baltimore, Druid Hall, 700 acres, and Patterson's Park, 35¼ acres. San Francisco has twelve squares of small extent—one improved. Cincinnati, Washington Park, 4¼ acres; Lincoln Park, 7 acres; Hopkins, 1½ acre; City Park, 1½ acre; and Longworth's Garden of Eden, 156 acres. St. Louis, Tower Grove Park, $276\tfrac{76}{100}$ acres; it has also fourteen others, containing 119 acres, and Shaw's Garden, the wonder of the West,

(143)

276 acres. Chicago, Lincoln Park, 50 acres; Washington Park $2\frac{3}{10}$ acres; Lake Park, 40 acres; Dearborn Park, 1½ acre; Ellis Park, 3 acres; Union Park, 17 acres; Jefferson Park, 5½ acres; Vernon Park, 4 acres: in all, nearly 126 acres, in addition to the Riverside, 1600 acres. Boston, Common, 48 acres. New Haven, Wooster, 5 acres; the Green, 16 acres; the Brewster, 55 acres. Philadelphia, Hunting Park, 45 acres; Fairmount Park, 3160 acres. The other Philadelphia Parks, or Squares, are—Logan Square, 7 acres 3 roods; Franklin Square, 7 acres 3 roods; Rittenhouse Square, 6 acres 2 roods; Washington Square 6 acres 2 roods; Independence Square, 4 acres 2 roods; Jefferson Square, 2 acres 2 roods.

STATISTICS OF THE WATER DEPARTMENT.

Contents of the reservoirs:—

		Gallons.
Fairmount		26,996,636
Corinthian Avenue		37,300,000
Schuylkill (formerly Spring Garden)		9,800,000
Belmont		35,800,000
		109,896,636
Roxborough	11,407,567	
Germantown	2,083,875	
Delaware, old reservoir	9,284,000	
" new reservoir	13,000,000	
		35,775,442
All the reservoirs		145,672,078

Pumping capacity of the works, July, 1871:—

Fairmount (water-power), about		34,191,619
Schuylkill, about		22,947,000
Belmont, "		10,000,000
Per twenty-four hours		67,138,619
Roxborough	2,500,000	
Germantown	750,000	
Delaware	11,000,000	
		14,250,000
All the works		81,388,619

There are seven turbines and two breast wheels at Fairmount.

(145)

Water-level:—

Belmont reservoir, when full, 212 feet above city datum.
Corinthian Av. " " 120 " "
Schuylkill " " 120 " "
Delaware " " 114 " "
Fairmount " " 96 " "
Roxborough " " 365 " "

Have 488½ miles of distributing pipes.

The average daily supply for the month of July, 1870, was:—

From Fairmount	26,191,619
Schuylkill	10,404,431
Delaware	5,210,439
Belmont	3,424,059
Germantown	748,187
	46,008,735

Equal to $68\frac{3}{10}$ gallons for each of the population, per revised census, or $83\frac{25}{100}$ gallons for each of the population who receive a supply from the works, or 483 gallons per day for each water tenant.

The greatest supply delivered in any one day was on July 20, 1870, as follows:—

From Fairmount	29,921,539
Schuylkill	14,856,940
Delaware	5,135,750
Belmont	3,958,680
Germantown	781,600
	54,654,509

Equal to 81 gallons for the total population, or $92\frac{3}{10}$ gallons for the total population supplied by the works; or 540 gallons for each water tenant.

The supply delivered in the year 1850 was 18 gallons for each of population; in 1860, 48 gallons for each of population; and in 1870, 55 gallons for each of population.

The increase in population from 1850 to 1860 was 38 per cent., whilst the increase in supply of water was 62 per cent.

The increase in population from 1860 to 1870 was 19 per cent., whilst the increase in water-supply was 41 per cent.

Supply of water:—

	Gallons.	Population.
1820	1,537,200	119,325
1830	3,074,644	167,811
1840	4,922,257	225,359
1850	7,432,337	408,763
1860	27,345,176	565,592
1870	46,008,735	673,726

Population, 673,726; houses in the city, 115,132, equal $5\frac{99}{100}$ per house. There were, January 1, 1870, 98,792 dwellings in Philadelphia; at $5\frac{99}{100}$ per dwelling, would make the number of persons supplied 554,030, equal to $87\frac{8}{10}$ per cent. of the whole population who pay for the water.

The reservoir in the east Park will contain 750,000,000 gallons.

APPENDIX.

INEDITED LETTERS OF ROBERT MORRIS.

In 1794, Mr. Morris was President of the Asylum Company. He began, with John Nicholson, of this city, to invest largely in land in 1795. On the 20th February, 1795, the North American Land Company was formed by Morris, Nicholson, and James Greenleaf, of New York. The capital stock consisted of six millions and forty-three and one quarter acres of land, in Pennsylvania, Virginia, Kentucky, North Carolina, South Carolina, and Georgia. The fragments of this vast estate, collected by the late Mr. Dundas, as surviving manager of the company (1859), and long after all connected with it were ruined and dead, amounted to nearly a quarter of a million dollars. We are permitted to copy from the originals the following letters of Robert Morris; some from the Park and some from the Prune Street Jail; they have not heretofore been made public.

HILLS, Sept. 6, 1797.

JOHN NICHOLSON, ESQ.

DEAR SIR: Here is a morning that will *cool* you and your letters so quick, that I think you will dispatch the business they import, without further delay. Mr. Graham will of course soon have the letter you intended to prepare for him to be sent to the Board of Managers of the North American Land Company. I hope Jesse Sharpless may get to a hotter place than my warm house before he can make a successful attack on you. We are hard threatened, but I hope that care and vigilance will disappoint all of them as to our persons. Whether you were right about the yellow fever or not, is not yet determined amongst the doctors; and as to your being always right, I will not answer for the future, but for the past I answer, no. If you had, neither you or I should have been as we are. My Chestnut Street house and lot, these grounds (the Hills), and some ground-rents, are advertised by Mr. Baker for sale on the 15th inst., and what to do I am at a loss, not having heard from Allen, and not having time enough to write to and hear from Mr. Ashley, and whether he will be back in time is uncertain; so that I am in great distress, without as yet seeing relief at hand. If this thing takes place, it is of little consequence whether I am taken or not. As yet I am furnished with victuals, as formerly, by Jenny and a black cook, who does not come into the house, neither do any others, except my own family and such persons as I send for; except, also, that I admitted William Lewis, George Graham, and Hetty. I believe Hetty would like to come here if you could spare her, but this I do not ask. . . . . . . Can you assist me to raise $500 to send off Mr. Richard, otherwise his two years' labor will be lost. I have been scheming and trying, but without success. No man, it seems, can command—rather say, spare—so large a sum. Poor Sterett! poor Sheaff! What shall we do? Powerful exertions must be made, for, at all events, we must relieve all who have served us, and all who may continue to serve us. This day will drive the yellow fever away, and relieve you from the heat you complain of. With best wishes, I am,

Dear sir, your obedient servant,
ROBERT MORRIS.

HILLS, Oct. 25, 1797.

JOHN NICHOLSON, ESQ.

DEAR SIR: I am now possessed of your notes of this date, Nos. 1 to 6. I have received this day a notice from Greenleaf, that he has applied to the Justices of the Court of Common Pleas for liberation; you will find herein a copy of the notice sent to me; it is dated the 15th inst., and came to-day to my counting-house, with the curious indorsement on it in Mr. Elliott's handwriting. I shall take measures about my suits immediately. To No. 2, I say, O Kentucky, Kentucky! is there any faith in thy goodly lands? My assent is with your No. 3. . . . . . . While I am writing, I receive your further notes of to-day, Nos. 7, 8, 9. I wish to God these notes would serve to take up those that bear promise of payments! They are numerous already; but if they would answer the other purpose, you would want more copying-presses and half a dozen paper-mills. . . . . . . Your No. 8 I shall answer when I have more leisure. To No. 9, I answer, that they will have done advertising and selling our property after it is all sold and gone. 200,000 acres of my land in North Carolina, which cost me $27,000, is sold for one year's taxes. By Heaven, there is no bearing with these things! I believe I shall go mad. Every day brings forward scenes and troubles almost insupportable; and they seem to be accumulating, so that at last they will, like a torrent, carry everything before them. God help us! for men will not. We are abandoned by all but those who want to get from us all we yet hold. Your fellow-sufferer,

ROBERT MORRIS.

HILLS, Dec. 21, 1797.

JOHN NICHOLSON, ESQ.

DEAR SIR: I have received your letters, Nos. 4, 5, 6, and 7 of yesterday, and Nos. 1, 2, and 3 of this date. . . . . . To No. 2, I say, I will starve before I will do what is therein mentioned. . . . . . I send herewith the letter from the Trustees of the Aggregate Fund, dated the 20th, which came to me this day. Pray what security do they mean, when they say the security *we requested?* I do not recollect any request of a particular security in their letters, and to me none has been made verbally, although I believe it has to you. We must see each other on this business. I wish you were here now; I have a fine fire, and the night is so cold that the devil himself would not turn out to catch you going home. I have a choice of difficulties, and a number of troubles in various cases, but one that hits me hardest just now arises with Church and Hamilton in New York. Good heavens, what vultures men are in regard to each other! I never, in the days of prosperity, took advantage of any man's distresses, and I suppose what I now experience is to serve as a lesson whereby to see the folly of humane and generous conduct.

Yours,

ROBERT MORRIS.

HILLS, Jan. 22, 1798.

JOHN NICHOLSON, ESQ.

DEAR SIR: Yours, Nos. 1, 2, and 3, of this day, are just brought out. I see you had a busy day yesterday; I was very near adding one to the number of your visitors, but now I see it would have been of no use had I gone. . . . . . . I have written to John Cunningham to inform me all he can of the proceedings against my lands in Cunningham's district. As you are a great lawyer, I mean to consult you about that affair. He said also that similar proceedings, "he believed," were had against our lands under the management of Mr. Hoge, and against all your donation lands. So there is work cut out for both of us. . . . . . . There is a Frenchman intends to shoot me at the window if I do not pay a note he had protested on Saturday. I thank you for the paper inclosed in No. 3. The Secretary of the North American Land Company is here, and regrets that he was not in town when your note to him came there; he received it here.

ROBERT MORRIS.

HILLS, February 5, 1798.

DEAR SIR: I got safe here, and found it the only place of calmness and quiet my foot was in all yesterday. It has made me more averse to the city than ever, and I detest Prune Street more than ever; therefore, keep me from it, if possible, my dear friend.

ROBERT MORRIS.

To JOHN NICHOLSON, ESQ.

HILLS, Feb. 7, 1798.

JOHN NICHOLSON, ESQ.

DEAR SIR: I did not hear from you yesterday, so that I am not acquainted with what has been fixed with George Eddy, or what is doing with the creditors for whom he is my bail; neither has J. Baker been here. Is anything doing with his list of creditors? Is Samuel Jackson relieved of the necessity of giving bail, and Sterett the same? What is doing for John Allen? Is there any chance of saving my furniture from the sheriff, and my person from jail, or are these things fixed?

Yours, etc.,

ROBERT MORRIS.

P. S.—I have just received your letter of yesterday and its inclosures, and I read Prune Street in every line.

HILLS, Feb. 8, 1798.

JOHN NICHOLSON, ESQ.

DEAR SIR: I return herewith the letters and copies of letters received under cover of yours to me of the 6th inst., which are the last I have received from you. Although I am expecting to hear what kind of reception and answers your circular letter has met with, I cannot say that I have conceived the smallest degree of hope from that measure; on the contrary, I consider my fate as fixed: hard and cruel fate it is. The punishment of my imprudence in the use of my name, and loss of credit, is perhaps what *I* deserve, but it is, nevertheless, severe on my family, and on *their* account I feel it most tormentingly. On *their* account I would do anything to avert what I foresee must happen next week, except *an act that would still affect them more deeply.* I will try to see you before I go to prison, and in the mean time I remain your distressed friend,

ROBERT MORRIS.

THE FOLLOWING LETTERS ARE FROM THE PRUNE STREET JAIL:—

February 20, 1798.

To JOHN NICHOLSON, ESQ.

DEAR SIR: My confinement has, so far, been attended with disagreeable and uncomfortable circumstances; for, having no particular place allotted to me, I feel myself an intruder in every place in which I go. I sleep on other persons' beds, I occupy other people's rooms; and if I attempt to sit down to write, it is at the interruption and inconvenience of some one who has acquired a prior right to the place. I am trying daily to get a room for a high rent, and now have a prospect of succeeding. I am now writing in a room which is the best in the house, and hope to have complete possession in a day or two; then I can set up a bed, and introduce such furniture and conveniences as will make me comfortable.

February 21, 1798.

DEAR SIR: Your letters, Nos. 1 and 2 of yesterday, and No. 1 of this day, are before me. I have signed, sealed, and forwarded all the letters for the Trustees of the Aggregate Fund. But what shall we do for General Forest and Mr. Dunlop? Shall we give them a rider on the city property next to Jacob Baker. This would interest them to save it from destruction. Suppose you sound them on this point. I am yet in so unsettled a state here, that it is not pleasant to see anybody, although many have been to see me, some as complimentary visitors, others on business. I do not encourage either, because I mean to be master of my time, and to make what *I may think* the best use of it. As yet I have not the conveniences for doing business, and, perhaps, the less one does in such a situation the better. My little book of suits is yet at the Hills, as are a number of books and papers which must come here when I have a place in which they can be placed; but when that will be, God only knows, if he knows or concerns in anything that relates to prisons. By this, I do not mean any impiety; on the contrary, the expression of a doubt would appear to be justified by what you meet with in such places. . . . . . . Charles Young is at me here, but he behaves very well so far. Adieu. I am called to dinner, by which you may learn that we eat "even here." Your obedient servant.

ROBERT MORRIS.

JOHN NICHOLSON, ESQ.

July 5, 1798.

JOHN NICHOLSON, ESQ.

DEAR SIR: I have your three letters of yesterday, but as I made a frolic yesterday, I did not read them until this morning. At first I did not relish your letters to Law, Duncanson, and the Trustees; but, after a second and a third reading, I signed and shall transmit them all; those for Law and Duncanson open under cover to Cranch. I agree to Lovering as an arbitrator with Prentiss. I think you had as snug a frolic yesterday as Mr. Anybody, but I hope the future anniversaries of your birthdays will be numerous, and passed in full possession of liberty. I had a thought of writing in to Greenleaf about Duncanson's bills, but my soul revolted, and the right hand refused to perform its functions.

Fitzsimons was here this morning, in a dreadful taking. All the furniture must be sold. My family think this dreadful hard; they know the debt is not mine.

ROBERT MORRIS.

October 15, 1798, Monday morning.

DEAR SIR: I received yours of last evening just after Mr. Hofner had come in sick. Mrs. Morris and Maria were sitting with me. He was pale and ghastly, horror in his countenance, and, I fear, terror in his mind. He sent for a French doctor, a Mons. Monges, who came, but will not yet pronounce whether it is or is not the yellow fever. He, however, has a fever, had last evening two or three slight spells of vomiting, and now complains of pains in his bowels. These are bad symptoms, and I fear he has it. Mrs. M. and my daughter left me with fresh anxieties on their minds, for here is a woman, wife of the man that cleans my room, makes my bed, etc., was taken ill on Saturday. Under these aggravated circumstances, Mr. Banks and myself have written this morning to the chief justice, and Captain Broadhead is going instantly with the letters. It is wonderful, but, notwithstanding the danger is now at my chamber door—for Hofner is in the room I formerly occupied—I feel no kind of apprehensions, and my only anxiety is for my wife and daughter, and these poor sick people. I hope my life will be spared, for the sake of my family, until I get my affairs settled. I shall be glad that you tell me that Mrs. Nicholson is getting, and that you continue well, which will comfort

ROBERT MORRIS.

JOHN NICHOLSON, ESQ.

October 18, 1798.

JOHN NICHOLSON, ESQ.

DEAR SIR: As I have done everything in my power to get from hence, and have not succeeded, I now make up my mind to wait with composure my fate. Charles' wife is gone to the hospital. Hofner cannot be moved. His mother, I am told, thinks him past danger, but *Dr.*

Jacob says he will die, and tells me that Dr. Monges, after seeing him at 11 o'clock last night, said he despaired.

I think of moving out of my room into that formerly occupied by Dr. Ruston, in the back part of the house; if I do this, it is to give some comfort to Mrs. Morris, whose distress pierces my heart. As to myself, I cannot feel afraid or alarmed at the neighborhood of this disease, although I have tried. Yours truly,

ROBERT MORRIS.

JOHN NICHOLSON, ESQ.

October 18, 1798.

DEAR SIR: The scene is closed with Hofner; he is gone the journey from which no traveller returns. I am now quartered in Dr. Ruston's room, having just got there when the exit was announced. I hope we shall avoid infection, for, if once taken, there seems to be no escape.

Yours,

ROBERT MORRIS.

JOHN NICHOLSON, ESQ.

January 2, 1799.

JOHN NICHOLSON, ESQ.

DEAR SIR: I think this is the day appointed for the sale of the Hills furniture, and I have not been able to see Mr. Cazenove yet on that subject, but expect him to-day.

The year began with a terrible disappointment to me, as yesterday I received a letter from Messrs. Bourdieu & Co., telling me they could not accept my bill on them for £389 9*s*. 5*d*. sterling, because my moneys and effects in their hands had been attached by Mr. James Eyma, of Martinique, in consequence of his being holder of a bond in judgment from myself and Mr. Nicholson, in the sum of $7000. They believe the bond is in the hands of Paschall Neilson Smith, of New York, and if I can get them relieved of the attachment, they will gladly pay the bill, and lament that such an impediment should be in the way. This blow was unexpected; it is death to my hopes, for I was in daily expectation to receive the cash here, believing the bill would be paid. The bond in Mr. Eyma's possession is one of those we gave to James Seagrove for his Georgia lands, and I remember Mr. Smith applied to me for payment of the first instalment and interest, which neither you nor I could pay at the time, nor can we now, so that my money in London must go towards it; and in this, as in a thousand other instances, I must "grin and bear it." But what is to be done for subsistence? I counted on this as a means to carry me through 1799.

I hope you have cured your smoking chimney, that you have fuel, and the means to buy food and raiment for your family. I will make new exertions to attain the same for mine, and then, in despite of all disappointments, we will try and work cheerfully and arduously to ameliorate our situation. Prison bounds, if established, will do great things for us. That business progresses slowly, but we must not appear too active or openly in it, lest we injure instead of promoting it. McClenahan intends to make use of the bankrupt law, I am told, and therefore does not concern himself about prison bounds. I heard that Governor Mifflin is at the point of death, and am sorry for it. You are in my debt, I think, several letters or notes, such as they are, from

Yours, etc.,
ROBERT MORRIS.

August 7, 1799.

JOHN NICHOLSON, ESQ.

DEAR SIR: I return Mr. Ely's letter of this date to you, and the copy of your reply; these I received under cover of your favor of this date, and I send also a letter just now brought to me from Mr. Ely, who certainly wishes this affair was settled, but he cannot lose sight of his (expected) profits. You see he cannot forget "Shylock;" indeed, he does not act up to the character, being willing to abate of the pound of flesh, but the part he does require calls for blood with it, and more than we can spare, unless our veins were replenished from some of those sources that used formerly to supply them so copiously. Mr. Ely seems disposed to make a settlement in the Genesee country, but he does not offer his debt for land, and if he did, I could not give him any in that country, as it is all involved in—puzzle the cause—I stopped here to answer Mr. Ely; you will receive it herewith, and, if approved, I must trouble you to seal and send it to him. I am sorry to learn that you are still beset; you must look out sharp, and keep from hence, except on Sundays.

ROBERT MORRIS.

The first commitment was made out for Robert Morris 18th January, 1798, and in February he was in prison.

The late William B. Wood describes him as he first saw him in the prison-yard: "His dress, a little old-fashioned, was adjusted with care; he returned my salutation in silence; he continued his walk, dropping from his hand, at a given spot, a pebble on each round, until a certain number which he had in his hand were exhausted." He remained four years, 1798–1802, in this jail. His will, made in 1804, two years after his release, thus concludes:—

"Here I have to express my regrets at having lost a very large fortune acquired by honest industry, which I had long hoped and expected to enjoy with my family during my own life, and then to distribute it among those of them that should outlive me. Fate has determined otherwise, and we must submit to the decree, which I have endeavored to do, with patience and fortitude."

He died May 8, 1806, aged 73 years.

TABLE OF DISTANCES.

FROM FAIRMOUNT.

To Girard Avenue Bridge	1 mile.
" Lansdowne Entrance	1¼ "
" Lansdowne	2¼ miles.
" George's Hill, direct	3½ "
" " " *via* Belmont	4½ "
" Belmont, direct	3½ "
" " *via* George's Hill	4½ "
" Mount Prospect, *via* Belmont	4½ "
" " " George's Hill	5¾ "
" The Falls, *via* River Road	4½ "
" " " George's Hill	6½ "
" The Wissahickon, *via* River Road	5½ "
" " " " George's Hill	7¼ "
" " " " East Bank	4 "
From the Falls to Wissahickon	1 mile.
To Maple Spring Hotel	1¼ "
" The Pipe Bridge	4¼ miles.
" Valley Green	4¾ "
" The First Fountain	5¼ "
" Indian Rock	5¾ "
" Thorp's Mill Road	7 "
" Chestnut Hill	7½ "

RULES AND REGULATIONS.

SECTION I.—*Penal.*

1. No person shall drive or ride in Fairmount Park at a rate exceeding seven miles an hour.

2. No one shall ride or drive therein upon any other part of the Park than upon the avenues and roads.

3. No vehicle of burden or traffic shall pass through the Park.

4. No person shall enter or leave the Park except by such gates or avenues as may be for such purpose arranged.

5. No coach or vehicle used for hire shall stand upon any part of the Park, for the purpose of hire.

6. No person shall indulge in any threatening, abusive, insulting, or indecent language in the Park.

7. No person shall engage in any gaming, nor commit any obscene or indecent act, in the Park.

8. No person shall carry fire-arms or shoot birds in the Park, or within fifty yards thereof, or throw stones or other missiles therein.

9. No person shall disturb the fish or water-fowl in the pool or pond, or birds in any part of the Park, or annoy, strike, injure, maim, or kill any animal kept by the direction of the Commissioners, either running at large or confined in a close; nor discharge any fireworks, nor affix any bills or notices therein.

10. No person shall cut, break, or in any wise injure or deface the trees, shrubs, plants, turf, or any of the buildings, fences, bridges, structures, or statuary, or foul any fountains or springs within the Park.

11. No person shall throw any dead animal or offensive matter or sub-

stance of any kind, into the river Schuylkill, within the boundaries of Fairmount Park.

12. No person shall go in to bathe within the Park.

13. No person shall turn cattle, goats, swine, horses, dogs, or other animals loose into the Park.

14. No person shall injure, deface, or destroy any notices, rules, or regulations for the government of the Park, posted or in any other manner permanently fixed by order or permission of the Commissioners of Fairmount Park within the limits of the same.

Any person who shall violate any of said Rules and Regulations shall be guilty of a misdemeanor, and for each and every such offence shall pay the sum of five dollars, to be recovered before any Alderman of the city of Philadelphia, as debts of that amount are recoverable, which fines shall be paid into the City Treasury, for Park purposes.

SECTION II.—*Licenses.*

1. No person shall expose any article for sale within the Park, without the previous license of the Park Commissioners.

2. No person shall have any musical, theatrical, or other entertainment therein, nor shall any military or other parade or procession, or funeral, take place in or pass through the limits of the Park, without the license of the Park Commissioners.

3. No gathering or meeting of any kind, assembled through advertisement, shall be permitted in the Park without the previous permission of the Commissioners.

4. No person shall engage in any play at base-ball, cricket, shinney, foot-ball, croquet, or at any other games with ball and bat, nor shall any foot-race or horse-race be permitted within the limits of the Park, except on such grounds only as shall be specially designated for such purpose.

5. No person shall take ice from the Schuylkill within the Park, without the license of the said Commissioners first had, upon such terms as they may think proper.

6. No person shall be permitted to use the shores of the river Schuylkill within the boundaries of Fairmount Park as a landing-place for boats, or keep thereat boats for hire, nor floating boat-houses with pleasure-boats for hire, except by special license or lease granted by the Commissioners, to be paid for as the Commissioners shall from time to time direct, and only at places designated by and under restrictions determined upon by said Commissioners.

7. No regatta or boat-race by boat-clubs, whose houses are built upon any part of the Park grounds, shall take place within the boundaries of the Park without special permission granted by the Commissioners, or by their Committee on Superintendence and Police.

8. Every boat or skating club, whose house or building is built on Park grounds, shall be required to obtain a license or lease from the Commissioners, on such terms and under such restrictions as the Commissioners shall determine.

SECTION III.—*Prohibitions.*

1. No gathering or meeting for political purposes in the Park shall be permitted under any circumstances.

2. No intoxicating liquors shall be allowed to be sold within said Park.

SECTION IV.—*Duties of Park-Guard or Police.*

1. It shall be the duty of the Park-Guard or Police appointed to duty in the Park, without warrant, forthwith to arrest any offender against the preceding rules and regulations, whom they may detect in the commis-

sion of such offence, and to take the person or persons so arrested forthwith before a magistrate having competent jurisdiction.

2. It shall be the duty of the Park-Guard or Police appointed to duty in the Park, at the termination of each week, to make a written report to the Committee on Superintendence and Police of all infractions of these rules and regulations, the number of arrests made, the nature of each offence, the name of the magistrate before whom each offender was taken, and the amounts of fines imposed and paid in each case.

By order of the Commissioners of Fairmount Park.

INSTRUCTIONS FOR THE PARK-GUARD.

1. Neatness in dress, propriety in speech and demeanor, perfect sobriety, obliging manners, and courtesy towards every visitor of the Park, are essential requisites for a satisfactory discharge of the duties of the Guard.

2. The uniform of the Guard being furnished by the Commissioners, it is only to be worn when on duty, and is to be kept in a cleanly and tidy condition.

3. The Guard is expected to render all possible aid and assistance in case of accidents to pedestrians, horsemen, or carriages, and particularly to protect females and children against every kind of annoyance, rudeness, or insult from evil-disposed and disorderly persons.

4. Whilst the Guard is expected to repress every kind of disorder and misconduct on the part of visitors, and to arrest those who are clearly guilty of an intentional violation of the rules and regulations ordained for the government and protection of the Park, great care is recommended not to become over-meddlesome, and thereby create instead of avoiding disorder.

5. Arrests should only be made when either the Guard himself or some respectable person at hand can testify to a malicious violation of the rules and regulations.

6. No arrest should be made for mere trifling violations, when a quiet reminder or reprimand would suffice to prevent a repetition of the offence.

7. Great indulgence is recommended towards children; but discreet, dignified, yet firm and decisive action towards gangs of unruly boys.

8. No officer of the peace should ever disgrace his position by abusing his authority, or by the exercise of tyranny make himself a terror to well-disposed citizens.

9. The Guard will remember that they are numbered, to enable any respectable person to complain of their misconduct, which, when clearly established, will lead to their immediate dismissal.

10. The Guard is required to make faithfully the weekly written report prescribed by the rules, and hand the same to the Chairman of the Committee on Superintendence and Police, stating at the same time all complaints made by respectable persons concerning inconveniences or annoyances in the Park.

11. The Guard is under the immediate direction of the Committee on Superintendence and Police. The Guard is required to obey the orders of the Chief Engineer of the Park. Such as are stationed near the Fairmount Water Works, or near any other water works of the city of Philadelphia, will duly respect the orders of the Chief Engineer of Water Works touching the property belonging to his department within the Park.

12. In cases of emergency, the Park-Guard is subject to the orders of the Mayor of the city of Philadelphia.

13. The Park-Guard is required to be on duty from 7 A.M. till sunset, during the months of May, June, July, August, September, and October. Those of the Guard who are on duty during the night, are required to report themselves half an hour before the day Guard is relieved.

14. Every member of the Guard is bound to report in person at least once during every twenty-four hours, at the office of the Chief Engineer, situated within the limits of the Park.

15. In case of sickness or other unavoidable inability to attend to his duty, every member of the Guard is required to have the fact immediately reported at the office of the Chief Engineer.

16. Room will be provided near the Chief Engineer's office for the convenience of the Guard to put on and take off the Guard uniform.

By order of the Committee on Superintendence and Police.

HALL & CARPENTER,

No. 709 Market Street,

PHILADELPHIA,

AGENTS FOR THE

AMERICAN SCREW CO.'S

WARRANTED RIVETS AND BOLTS.

AGENTS FOR THE SALE OF

AMERICAN SPELTER

AND

SHEET ZINC.

HALL & CARPENTER,

No. 709 Market Street,

PHILADELPHIA.

IMPORTERS OF AND DEALERS IN

TIN PLATE AND METALS,

BLACK AND GALVANIZED SHEET IRON,

Russia and Patent Planished Iron,

WIRE

OF ALL KINDS,

Sheet and Bolt Copper,

HOT AIR REGISTERS.

CLAXTON, REMSEN & HAFFELFINGER,
Publishers, Booksellers and Stationers,
Nos. 624, 626 & 628 Market Street, Philadelphia.

The Zoological Gardens are open from 10 A. M. to 7 P. M., including Sundays. During the summer, there is music on Wednesday and Saturday afternoons, while in winter there is frequently skating on the lake. The display of animals, etc., is most attractive and complete.

Admission, Adults, 25 cents.   Children, under ten years, 10 cents.

THE SCHUYLKILL NAVY.

ORGANIZED OCTOBER, 1858.

OFFICERS:

JAMES M. FERGUSON, Commodore.

JOHN HOCKLEY, Jr., Vice-Commodore.

J. GILLINGHAM, Secretary.

F. W. MURPHY, Treasurer.

The Schuylkill Navy propose holding a series of Regattas during July, 1876, as follows:

First—The National Association will be invited to hold their Annual Regatta of that year on the Schuylkill River, and in addition to the regular prizes of the association the Schuylkill Navy will present special prizes of flags and individual gold medals to the winning crews.

Second—The College Clubs have been invited to hold their Annual Regatta of that year at Philadelphia; a piece of plate to be presented to the winners, in addition to individual gold medals.

Third—An International College Race for four-oared shells will be held, the prize to be a valuable piece of plate with gold medals to the winning crews.

Fourth—An International Race will be held, open to all regularly organized boat clubs throughout the world, to be rowed in accordance with the rules of the National Amateur Rowing Association of the United States, the prizes to be first and second for fours, pairs, and single and double sculls; and, in addition, a medal to be presented to each man rowing in the race; for the winning crews to be of gold; second boats of silver, and the remainder of bronze.

Fifth—A Professional Race, open to all crews, will be held for four-oared shells, the prize to be a purse of $2000 or more. All the expense of the regatta will be borne by the Schuylkill Navy, and they will make all arrangements for housing the boats, and provide proper dressing-rooms for all crews competing.

The President or presiding officer and Secretary of each club entering either of the amateur races or regatta controlled by the Schuylkill Navy will be required to certify on honor, in writing, that each member of the crew entered is strictly an amateur, and is not paid directly or indirectly for his services as a member, or by reason of his being a member of the club, that he "does not enter in open competition for either a stake, public or admission-money or entrance-fee, or compete with or against a professional for any prize, and has never taught, pursued, or assisted in the pursuit of athletic exercises as a means of livelihood, or has been employed in or about boats, or in manual labor on the water."

Some of the above prizes have already been pledged, and an Honorary Committee is being organized from our best citizens, as well as from other parts of the country, who will aid the Schuylkill Navy in making this the grandest Regatta ever held in the world. Any one wishing to aid in this enterprise or obtain information concerning it can do so by calling on any of the officers.

JOHN BAIRD, SONS & CO.,

IMPORTERS OF

Italian Goods, Marble,

AND RAGS,

No. 214 South Twenty-Fourth Street,

PHILADELPHIA.

JOHN BAIRD.	THOS. E. BAIRD.
WM. M. THOMAS.	JOHN E. BAIRD.

United States International Exhibition.

Subscriptions to the Stock of the International Exhibition received by

FREDERICK FRALEY,

No. 904 Walnut Street, Philadelphia.

TEN DOLLARS PER SHARE.

$UBSCRIBERS taking Five Shares will pay only 40 per cent. of the amount in cash, balance in nine months.

Each subscription of Ten Dollars will be receipted for by a Superb Line Engraving Certificate, executed in the United States Treasury Department.

Fac-Simile of Centennial Memorial Medal.

OBVERSE.

REVERSE.

ISSUED BY THE

CENTENNIAL BOARD OF FINANCE,

904 WALNUT STREET,

UNDER THE AUTHORITY OF THE UNITED STATES GOVERNMENT.

IN order that the cost of the Medals might be brought within reach of all, they are of three descriptions:

In Gilt	$5 00
In Silver	3 00
In Bronze	2 00

The Illustrations approximate in size the first and third mentioned; the second is the size of the American Dollar. The design of the "Obverse," represents on all, the Genius of American Independence, rising from a recumbent position, grasping with her right hand the sword which is to enforce her demands, and raising her left, in appealing pride to the galaxy of thirteen stars, indicating the original Colonies. The "Reverse" displays the Genius of Liberty, with the sword buckled to her girdle, at rest. With either hand extends a welcome and a chaplet to the Arts and Sciences assembled, with evidences of their skill and craft, to do honor to the Centennial.

FOR SALE BY

AGENTS IN ALL THE STATES,

And at No. 904 Walnut Street.

THE CENTENNIAL FOUNTAIN

TO BE UNVEILED IN

FAIRMOUNT PARK, PHILADELPHIA,

JULY 4, 1876,

UNDER THE AUSPICES OF

The Catholic Total Abstinence Union
OF AMERICA.

CHARLES CARROLL, ARCHBISHOP CARROLL, MOSES, BARRY, FATHER MATTHEW.

NOW being executed by H. Kirn, in Tyrolese Marble. The central figure is fifteen feet high—each of the four others is nine feet—the height to crown of central figure is 35 feet, and diameter of Fountain 100 feet. Amount of Marble in the entire work 6584 cubic feet.

Subscriptions of any amount may be forwarded to DR. MICHAEL O'HARA, Chairman of Centennial Committee, No. 31 South 16th Street, Philadelphia, or to the President of any Catholic Total Abstinence Society of the Union in the United States. A finely executed Heliotype of this Fountain will be forwarded to each subscriber on receipt of his subscription. The size for subscribers of One Dollar is 7x10 inches, now ready for delivery.

UNITED STATES
1776—INTERNATIONAL EXHIBITION.—1876

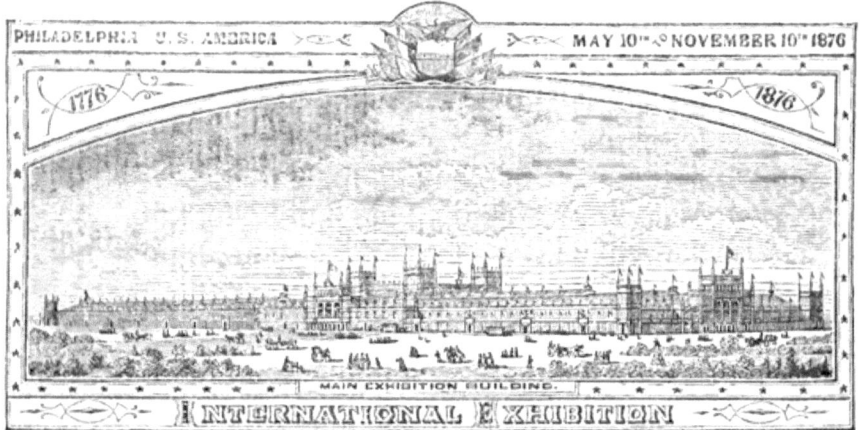

EXHIBITION OPENS MAY 10, 1876.
EXHIBITION CLOSES NOV. 10, 1876.

The following countries will exhibit: The German Empire, Great Britain, France, Austria, Sweden, Norway, The British Colonies—Canada, Australia, New Zealand, Tasmania, and others of the Australasian Islands, Peru, United States of Columbia, Nicaragua, The Argentine Confederation, Brazil, Venezuela, Ecuador, Chili, Guatemala, Salvador, Mexico, Honduras, Hayti, The Netherlands, Belgium, Liberia, the Sandwich Islands, China, Japan, Switzerland, Spain, the United States Government, and the States of the United States.

APPLICATIONS FOR SPACE.

To secure space for exhibits in the buildings of the Park, early application should be made. The necessary forms for application, together with the Regulations for Exhibitors and needed information, will be forwarded on application to the office of the Centennial Commission.

A. T. GOSHORN,
Director General,
904 Walnut St., Philada.

J. L. CAMPBELL,
Secretary.

www.ingramcontent.com/pod-product-compliance
Lightning Source LLC
Chambersburg PA
CBHW021728220426
43662CB00008B/760